The Solitudes

PENGUIN (Penguin) CLASSICS

LUIS DE GÓNGORA

The Solitudes

A DUAL-LANGUAGE EDITION WITH
PARALLEL TEXT

Translated with a Foreword and Notes by
EDITH GROSSMAN

Introduction by
ALBERTO MANGUEL

PENGUIN BOOKS

PENGUIN BOOKS

Published by the Penguin Group
Penguin Group (USA) Inc.,
375 Hudson Street, New York, New York 10014, U.S.A.
Penguin Group (Canada), 90 Eglinton Avenue East, Suite 700,
Toronto, Ontario, Canada M4P 2Y3
(a division of Pearson Penguin Canada Inc.)
Penguin Books Ltd, 80 Strand, London WC2R 0RL, England
Penguin Ireland, 25 St Stephen's Green, Dublin 2,
Ireland (a division of Penguin Books Ltd)
Penguin Books Australia Ltd, 250 Camberwell Road,
Camberwell, Victoria 3124, Australia
(a division of Pearson Australia Group Pty Ltd)
Penguin Books India Pvt Ltd, 11 Community Centre,
Panchsheel Park, New Delhi – 110 017, India
Penguin Group (NZ), 67 Apollo Drive, Rosedale, Auckland 0632,
New Zealand (a division of Pearson New Zealand Ltd)
Penguin Books (South Africa) (Pty) Ltd, 24 Sturdee Avenue,
Rosebank, Johannesburg 2196, South Africa

Penguin Books Ltd, Registered Offices:
80 Strand, London WC2R 0RL, England

This translation first published in Penguin Books 2011

1   3   5   7   9   10   8   6   4   2

Translation, foreword, and notes copyright © Edith Grossman, 2011
Introduction copyright © Alberto Manguel, 2011
All rights reserved

Introduction published by arrangement with Alberto Manguel,
c/o Guillermo Schavelzon & Asociados, S.L., Barcelona

ISBN 978-0-14-310638-8

Printed in the United States of America
Set in Sabon

Contents

Foreword

Certain figures in literary history take on an iconic quality and appear to represent and even illuminate moments of extreme importance in the development of a specific genre. In retrospect, their work seems to be the inescapable next step in the growth of an art form, though at the time they were writing no one could predict what direction that art form might take, and they were often attacked harshly for their deviation from the vision of earlier artists.

Luis de Góngora is such a figure. In hindsight, the arc of lyric poetry from Garcilaso de la Vega (1503–1536) to Luis de Góngora (1561–1627) in Renaissance Spain seems inevitable. Both poets were highly experimental writers—explorers, really, of poetic terra incognita. Early in the sixteenth century, Garcilaso, who like many other Renaissance writers assiduously composed classical verse in the style of Virgil and Horace, had an enormous impact on the trajectory of poetry in Spain by successfully hispanicizing Petrarchan forms, meters, and themes, effecting the import from Italy with so much skill they seemed native-born, and confirming indisputably and for all time the high aesthetic value of Italianate poetry within the Spanish poetic tradition. By the time Góngora began to write, the Petrarchan style had become so firmly entrenched, not only in Spanish but in all of European literature, that it was virtually inescapable. Continuing in Garcilaso's footsteps, however, Góngora also composed perfect little ballads and songs in traditional native meters. For these, he was dubbed the Prince of Light.

Góngora was born into a flourishing period of pan-European literary mannerism. In Spain, the turn away from a neoclassical aesthetic while simultaneously maintaining the forms of that aesthetic led to some startling work. For many years, the conventional view of Góngora found in literary histories was that his complex, hyperbolic, allusive, and highly metaphorical poetry was the result of mental disturbance. He was clearly insane, they said. He had to be to stray so far from the cultivated, tasteful, pellucid poetic of an earlier time. Or, ventured some, he was actually a clandestine Jew, the only way, they thought, to explain his fondness for a poetic style so un-Spanish in its intention, so contrary to the values of the Counter-Reformation. In a construct that recalls the schizophrenic fantasy of Jekyll and Hyde, for his longer poems, including the *Soledades*, or *Solitudes*, Góngora was called the Prince of Darkness.

What exactly did he do to provoke so virulent a response? The great poetic triumvirate of the time—Góngora, Quevedo, and Lope de Vega—were caustic enemies, making public verbal attacks on one another in widely circulated poems that insulted and accused rivals of dereliction, deviance, perversion, and endless, unspeakable crimes. The only thing Quevedo and Lope agreed on was how bitterly they both despised Góngora and what was called *culteranismo* or *cultismo* ("learnedism")—the poetic style of his *Fábula de Polifemo y Galatea*, for example, and of the *Soledades*. In fact, it has been claimed (though not proven) that Quevedo edited the limpid poems of Fray Luis de León in order to demonstrate, in a direct assault on Góngora, the exquisite clarity of the earlier poet's writing.

I believe that one of the things Góngora did with utter virtuosity, to the undying loathing of his contemporaries, was carry to its extreme, logical conclusion the artifice of the Petrarchan perception. In his "dark" writing, he stripped poetry of its emotional burden, severing its connection to representationalism and leaving only the pure aesthetic of language and metaphor. *The Solitudes* is a poem "about" nature, but the natural world in this work does not serve as the backdrop for a highly expressive love poem or spiritual meditation. It is there to be evoked for its own sake in the most rarefied, figurative, sensuous language because language itself, not its emotive referent or expressive content, is the intrinsic aesthetic component of poetry. This notion informs most poetic composition to some degree—it accounts for reflections upon the art as opposed to the subject matter in any consideration of the genre—but Góngora's rejection of figurative realism as a guiding standard for his work is absolute. It probably accounts for the attraction his writing held for Symbolist and Modernist poets of the nineteenth century and for avant-garde Spanish poets of the 1920s, who found in him a consummate antidote to bourgeois romanticism in all its guises (Pedro Salinas famously called him a "mystic of material reality"). The modern reevaluation of Góngora's reputation and the elevated status he enjoys today can be traced directly to the celebration in 1927 of the tricentenary of his death. The young poets of the time—among them Federico García Lorca, Vicente Aleixandre, Pedro Salinas, Luis Cernuda, and Dámaso Alonso, who was also a brilliant scholar and critic—embraced and honored Góngora's poetry, and the acclaim surrounding his name since then has not faded.

The Solitudes has approximately two thousand lines. Four sections were planned initially, but Góngora completed only the first, with 1091 lines, and 979 lines of the second, unfinished part. It is written in a standard random alternation of seven- and eleven-syllable lines called the *silva*, in stanzas of variable length. I have done my best to duplicate the meter (in Spanish verse, meter is determined by the number of syllables in a line, not by the number of feet, as in English). This means that in the translation, a seven-syllable line in Spanish has its counterpart in a seven-syllable line in English, and the same is true for the eleven-syllable lines, though on occasion I exchange meters, using, for example, a heptasyllable in English to translate a Spanish hendecasyllable. Regardless of these changes, I have maintained the heptasyllabic and hendecasyllabic meters. What I did not attempt to bring over into English is the rhyme. As I have said elsewhere, this is undoubtedly barbaric, since rhyme is so intrinsic to the rhythm of a poem, but

I would rather sacrifice that important structural element than create a piece of writing that sounds forced. In Spanish, as in Italian, rhymes are to be had almost for the asking; they are much more difficult to come by in English—for me, at least. Of course, when a rhyme or half rhyme occurred naturally or spontaneously in the course of translating, I relished it. Finally, for this translation I have used the groundbreaking edition of Dámaso Alonso (not the newest edition, but one I love dearly) and his indispensable prose version and explication of the poem, which is the source of many of my notes.

I hope that awareness of this extraordinary work helps to expand English-language readers' perceptions of Spanish literature, its poetry in particular, for it is startling to consider how little knowledge there is of Góngora in the English-speaking world. He is a major figure in the panorama of literature in Spanish and in the development of European poetry, but he has not escaped the great wall erected around all things Spanish in the sixteenth and seventeenth centuries, for essentially geopolitical reasons, by the French and English creation of the Black Legend of peninsular cruelty and obscurantism, and by Spain's own diligent contributions to that same myth for close to five hundred years.

Despite all dire forecasts regarding the imminent demise of the book, I believe there is a hunger for the kind of sustenance that can be found in great writing—even great writing that is several centuries old—even great writing that first appeared in another language. That is the real reason and justification for this translation of a poem that has intrigued me ever since I was a graduate student.

EDITH GROSSMAN

Note: The numbers assigned to lines in the English version of the poem do not always correspond to the line numbers in the Spanish original. This is due to syntactical differences between the two languages as well as the demands of translating poetic meter. By the same token, the number of lines in a particular stanza may not be the same in Spanish and English.

Introduction

The fluctuating fate of certain writers seems to depend not as much on their work itself (which, after all, remains more or less unchanged throughout the centuries) as on the expectations of their readers, on the notions these readers have of what literature should or should not do. Depending on who we are, and where and when we read, a given text will appear to have been written in one of two different kinds of language, or, rather, with what one might call different attitudes toward language. In the first, language seems to hide behind the story, to work unnoticed in the background of what is being said; in the second, language takes center stage and shows itself off with all its flourishes and trappings. Though most texts rely on a safe balance between the two, this ongoing tension between language invisible and language apparent mirrors not only our aesthetic but also our ethical and political imaginations.

Because we see in literature what we want or need to see, especially in literature that demands an effort of investigation and reflection, the fate of Luis de Góngora y Argote has been a succession of exaltations and denigrations. He was called by his contemporaries "the Spanish Homer"[1] and also the perpetrator of "Pestilential Poetry,"[2] he was ignored by the Romantics and rescued by the Modernists,[3] he deeply influenced poets as different as Stéphane Mallarmé and Federico García Lorca, and novelists such as Gabriel García Márquez and Juan Goytisolo. Jorge Luis Borges, not the dullest of readers, expressed, throughout his life, both a fervent devotion and an equally fervent aversion to Góngora, depending on how the master's overwhelming style suited Borges's own.

In his time—late sixteenth-century and early seventeenth-century Spain—Góngora was considered both the greatest of poets and a pretentious fool who squandered his poetic gifts on deliberately abstruse conceits. His mastery of portentous imagery and rhetorical devices, his disrespect for the conventional limits of serious literature, his interest in the everyday, banal reality of the world around him, irritated his rivals, and helped stir the animosity of his two greatest opponents, Lope de Vega and Francisco de Quevedo, who nevertheless expressed their admiration for his genius.

To degrade Góngora's style, his enemies invented the term *culteranismo*, which associates the notion of *culto*, affectedly cultivated, with *luteranismo*, Luther's heretic doctrines. *Conceptismo*, the opposing school, was led by Quevedo, and was supposed to dwell on literary wordplay and wit rather than on the intricacies of form. This established opposition, though certainly true in the personal dealings of its members, is less evident in their literary production: Quevedo's poetry can be exquisitely convoluted and Góngora's of heartbreaking plainness. Those who imagine Góngora's verse to be a thicket of impenetrable artifice might be unwilling to believe that these limpid lines are also his:

> Carthage confesses it. And you will not?
> You are in danger, Licius, if you insist
> on chasing shadows and embracing masks.
>
> No mercy from the hours should you expect,
> the hours that are grinding down the days,
> the days that keep on gnawing at the years.[4]

Luis de Góngora y Argote was the son of a noted lawyer and bibliophile from Córdoba. After a rowdy youth spent in Salamanca, he received, thanks to his father, an ecclesiastical benefice that allowed him to travel frequently throughout Spain. He finally settled in the Madrid court of Philip III, where, with the support of his patron, the Duke of Lerma, he became the royal chaplain. During this time, Góngora wrote a large number of classical sonnets and popular, humorous songs, several of which were published in two anthologies of contemporary poets that made him well known among the lettered classes. Then, reaching the age of fifty and feeling that court life was becoming increasingly hostile, he moved to Andalusia and, from 1609 to 1617, lived in almost complete isolation in a country house near Córdoba. Here Góngora began writing poetry of a much greater linguistic complexity than before, taking to almost unthinkable extremes the tenets of baroque poetry.

Though it is impossible to say why and how a poet alters his voice, an inkling of explanation might be found in the disillusioned political climate of Spain in the first decades of the 1600s. During the previous century, Spain had invented for itself several different official identities. It was the imperial power par excellence, conqueror of the seas and discoverer of the New World, of which, thanks to the Treaty of Tordesillas, it possessed the lion's share. It was a nation of pure Christian blood, having taken over the province of Granada and expelled both Jews and Arabs from its territories. It was the true defender of the Christian faith and the papal authority, a steadfast bastion against the Protestant Reformation. As a consequence, according to the nineteenth-century novelist Benito Pérez Galdós, "traditional hypocrisy served to cover up moral meanness, and corruption of the soul was transformed by priestly art into virtue and spiritual fortitude."[5]

To maintain this triple mask, Spain developed, in various exaggerated manifestations, a complex baroque style in which language itself appears to be the main protagonist of the text and also its justification, allowing the words to enclose and occlude what they are meant to reveal, sometimes to the point of annihilation. The Cuban novelist Severo Sarduy noted that the traditional etymology of "baroque" stems from the Portuguese term *barroco* used to designate an irregular pearl; eventually, the elaborate jewel made from that pearl (the artifact, the jeweler's handicraft) superseded the natural creation it was meant to name and acquired a connotation of artificiality rather than craftsmanship, and intricacy rather than depth.[6]

The baroque opposed, with its ornamentation and bombast, the plain tone of ordinary discourse and also the measured rules of sober classicism. It was a style ideally suited for the purposes of the Counter-Reformation: ideologically, it served to withdraw from public inspection the tenets of the Catholic dogma by surrounding and layering them until they effectively disappeared from view; aesthetically, to elevate, through artifice and conceit, the subjects of art and poetry so as not to confuse what is basely human with the aspirations of the divine. For precisely these reasons, the Reformation, in England, for instance, had stripped the altars and reduced worship to its simplest, barest form. In 1667, several decades after the baroque had established itself in the Spanish peninsula, Bishop Sprat denounced from his pulpit in London the outrage of the baroque style, and explained why the Royal Society was determined to suppress its appearance in Protestant Britain:

> They have therefore been most rigorous in putting in execution the only Remedy that can be found for this extravagance, and that has been a constant Resolution to reject all amplifications, digressions, and swellings of style; to return back to the primitive purity and shortness, when men deliver'd so many *things* almost in an equal number of words.[7]

Amplifications, digressions, and swellings of style: these were the sins the critics of the baroque attributed to its practitioners, and, together with elegant wordplay, syntactic conceits, grammatical infringements, and all manner of rhetorical devices, they became the essential components of baroque language. Góngora exacerbated these almost to the point of parody. Metaphors, similes, and allegories were an essential part of a baroque construction, stretching as far as possible the terms of comparison; for his part, Góngora protracted his metaphors to such an extent that the described object became almost lost in a whirlwind of complex images. With uncanny virtuosity, Góngora constructed edifices of words that presented but did not replicate or mirror his intended subjects.

Dámaso Alonso, perhaps Góngora's most passionate defender, spoke of the landscape in Góngora's poetry as one that is "aesthetically transformed." Certainly, it is the nature of the countryside Góngora knew, but changed through his images into a mosaic of crystal, precious stones, silk, feathers, and brocades; his bodies are human, no doubt, but in his verse they have become roses, ivory, ebony, pearls. It is obvious that Góngora demonstrates, as few other poets, an absolute trust in the creative powers of language: he does not use words merely to name or echo reality; he uses them to reconstruct reality according to his poetic eye and ear. In some sense, his is the absolute act of translation: that of taking not a verbal construction but a material one and transforming it into something perfectly equivalent and yet utterly separate.

At this point, an example may be useful. Alluding to the poetic convention that spring is the season of new things, Shakespeare, Góngora's contemporary, asks:

> "Who are the violets now
> that strew the green lap of the new come spring?"[8]

Góngora too uses this literary trope but only as a distant inspiration. In the first verses of *The Solitudes*, he transforms this poetic triteness into a marvelously convoluted depiction of astronomical time, mythological narrative, and a wealth of mixed metaphors. Spring is not mentioned; instead, we are told of the flowery season of the year in which the sun enters the constellation of Taurus, the bull, the beast into which Jupiter transformed himself to kidnap Princess Europa. This bull, his forehead armed with a crescent moon of horns, radiant through the effect of the rays of the sun that mingle with its bristles, seems to be grazing on stars that pale in his luminous presence, in heavenly fields as blue as sapphire:

> It was the flowering season of the year
> when Europa's false-hearted abductor
> —a half moon the weapons on his brow,
> the Sun's rays all the strands of his hair—
> oh bright glory of heaven,
> grazes on stars in fields of sapphire blue . . . (1–6)

It is obvious to most readers that the essence of these verses is not in the story but in the telling of the story, in the voluptuous verbal construction that somehow, through sounds and images, constructs a musical picture that, like a riddle, must be disentangled for sense. But this disentanglement is, as it were, a posthumous operation. The first, the immediate experience of the reader is one of pure verbal pleasure, an erotic play of tongue and ear before soliciting our intelligent reflection. This is not to say that Góngora is not telling anything: he is telling much, and most precisely. But he is not interested in delivering "so many *things* almost in an equal number of words." On the contrary, his interest lies in multiplying and magnifying the things he wants to say so as to extend their meaning in space and time. Spring is, certainly, as Shakespeare reminds us, the season in which all things bloom, but it is also the season of cosmic astrological changes, of transformations of the dark into the light, of renewed links between the different cosmic and earthly elements, of a reappraisal of quotidian sights such as flowers and sheep and fields and skies, of recalling ancestral memories of founding myths. All this, and more, come into play in Góngora's account.

To restructure and enrich the language he was using for poetic purposes, Góngora returned to the Latin roots of Spanish, which allowed him greater freedom of syntax and wordplay. Borges saw in this "nostalgia of Latin"[9] a destructive tendency. "Gongorism," Borges wrote, "was the attempt by grammarians urged by a plan to dislocate the Spanish sentence into Latin disorder, without wanting to understand that this disorder is merely apparent in Latin, and was to become effective among us through a lack of declensions."[10]

And yet, Góngora's excesses were not merely formal. While it is true that Spain used the rhetoric and style of the baroque for its own purposes, it is also true that Spanish writers, by and large, subverted them. Cervantes created with *Don Quixote* a reverse image of the Spain promoted by officialdom: the supposed author of the novel is Cide Hamete Benegeli, one of the converted Moors expelled from Spain in 1610, thus bringing back one of the forbidden cultures to the very core of his story. Like Cervantes, Góngora witnessed, throughout his life, the ups and downs of the Spanish Empire, from the victory of Lepanto and the annexing of Portugal to the defeat of the Armada and the forced peace with England. Lucid, critical, and disillusioned, Góngora too rejected Spain's attempt to invent for itself false identities. In this he was extraordinarily successful. In 1627, the year of his death, the Spanish Inquisition prohibited the sale of his poetry. Obviously, something had been read in the baroque edifice of Góngora's verse that gravely offended the official ear.

Rather than the supposed glory of the Empire, Góngora's subject, in *The Solitudes* above all, is the life outside the court, the everyday activities of peasants, fishermen, and shepherds, not the protagonists of an artificial pastoral novel but ordinary people leading ordinary lives. Like Cervantes, he also had no patience with the Empire's supposed aristocratic purity. One of his rustics in *The Solitudes* tells of the conquest of the New World in harsh, critical terms that recall denunciations such as Bartolomé de las Casas's *Brief Description of the Destruction of the Indies*, depicting the imperial enterprise as both a political and a moral failure. The *conquista*, according to Góngora, is due not to worthy ambitions but to greed, and Spain has not learned the lesson of King Midas, condemned to starvation because everything he touches turns to inedible gold.

> Greed sent second barks to a second pole
> in a new sea that offered him not only
> the beautiful white daughters of its shells,
> but murderous metals Midas never learned
> to possess successfully. (I, 430–434)

Certain critics[11] speak of "the temptation of the epic" in Góngora's great poems, notably in *The Solitudes*. If there was such a thing (and no doubt the epic is a recurrent temptation indulged in by Torquato Tasso, Milton, and other of his near contemporaries), then Góngora seems to have conceived a particular version of the epic, something more akin to a pilgrimage in a world not of fabulous dangers and prodigious events, but of ordinary things, a world outside the scope of the great cities, a world of laborers, fishermen, and peasants. Thus in *The Solitudes*, Góngora took the classical contrast between country and city, that commonplace of Latin poetry recovered by the Renaissance, and converted it into an epic of the quotidian. A contemporary defender of Góngora, Díaz de Rivas, suggested that "his intention is not to treat of pastoral things (these matters are accidental circumstances of the work's main purpose) but the pilgrimage of a Prince, a highly placed personage, his absence and the painful affects of his exile."[12]

The poem, Góngora himself explains in a letter, was imagined as four *Solitudes*; this has led readers to imagine a correspondence between each part (those that Góngora finished and those that he did not) and a different landscape, a different state of mind, or a different human age. What we know for certain is that Góngora completed the 37 lines of the dedication to the Duke of Bejar, the 1091 lines of the *First Solitude* and only 979 of the *Second Solitude*, all of which circulated in manuscript from about 1613, and were not published until fourteen years later. Of the supposed other two sections we know nothing.

Are *The Solitudes* incomplete or deliberately left open? It may be that, like other unfinished works such as Kafka's *The Castle* or Coleridge's *Kubla Khan*, the expectation of conclusion is ours, not the author's. The pilgrims in all three works (Coleridge's narrator can be read as a dream traveler) undertake a journey whose purpose is the journey itself, not the arrival. The Castle must remain unreachable, the vision of Xanadu incomplete, the travels of the shipwrecked wanderer must never end. In Góngora's poem, only the city that the pilgrim has left is a limited space, confined by its walls; the wilderness beyond it, sea and land, are infinite, more pagan than Christian, and its fruits will always be, like Midas's viands, useless in the greedy hands of conquerors.

If Góngora's poem has a subject, other than the ongoing exploration of the natural world and its inhabitants, then it is the construction of solitude, the search for that state of mind and body in which a person may find some kind of understanding and peace of mind. Though the quest carries echoes of prophetic Biblical literature and the crying in the wilderness, *The*

Solitudes are not jeremiads; they are not conceived as lamentations but rather as songs of praise for the wonders of the world encountered by the exile, from humble human artifacts such as a wooden bowl and fishing nets, to the return of the tired falcons at the end of the *Second Solitude*:

> Though idle, no less fatigued,
> on the glove came complaining
> the rapid whirlwinds from Norway. (943–945)

Another contemporary, Francisco de Córdoba, Abbot of Rute, noted that Góngora's poetry resembles "a talking picture" that represents, "as in a Flemish painting," a variety of human types and activities.[13] If so, *The Solitudes* paints a meticulously realistic picture of the natural world in which every character, every object, every landscape, presented through a mesh of metaphors and images, is essentially and vividly factual.

Except perhaps for the pilgrim himself. To suit the perfect search for solitude, Góngora's pilgrim has no specific identity: he is a man almost without qualities; his only known characteristics are the beauty of Jupiter's Ganymede, an amorous despondency caused by a "beloved enemy," and a silent curiosity. Unlike the usual protagonist of the "village versus court" trope that invariably privileges pastoral life, the pilgrim, though aware of the merits of the country, is incapable of forming part of any society, whether urban or rustic. Longingly searching for solitude, he seems unaware that he carries his solitude within him, like an attribute of his being, akin to the foreigner that Charles Baudelaire was to describe centuries later, a man who has no family, no friends, no country, and loves nothing but the clouds, "the marvelous clouds."[14] Part Góngora himself, part the reader, the pilgrim is in a sense a dual creature: his body travels through the realms of his exile while his mind travels through a different landscape, one constructed for him out of words and learned mythological references and sophisticated cultural codes. Only once does the pilgrim take an active part in the story: when he intervenes on behalf of the young lovers in the fisherman's hut, in the *Second Solitude*. Otherwise, he is merely a witness to the world that unfolds before him.

Not everything in Góngora is perfectly understandable for the reader today, not even in translation, which tends to ease complexities and clarify obscurities. This is partly because he sometimes wrote verses in which the sound of the majestic syllables overrides the need for sense, and partly because, even with the guidance of erudite notes, our poetic vocabularies are far poorer now than they were for his seventeenth-century readers. I don't think this matters. Borges, writing in 1925 about that other *culterano*, James Joyce, said that he wanted to appropriate for the author of *Ulysses* Lope de Vega's "respectful words" on Góngora: "Be what it may, I will always esteem and adore the divine genius of this Gentleman, taking from him what I understand with humility and admiring with veneration what I am unable to understand."[15]

I mentioned the virtues of translation when reading a difficult work. If a literary text is basically something made of certain words placed in a certain order, following or contravening certain grammatical laws, chosen for their sense but often mainly for their music, then what becomes of that text when it is stripped of all these things and rebuilt with other words, another grammar, a different music? Particularly, what becomes of a text such as Góngora's *Solitudes* when translated into another language, another perception of the world, another state of mind? Mysteriously, in a good translation, as if under a new skin, the work comes back to life.

In Latin America, Góngora influenced much of the writing of Sor Juana Inés de la Cruz, of Borges, and (in lesser measure) of Gabriel García Márquez. Above all, he is the "origin and source" of the great Cuban literature, that of Alejo Carpentier, Severo Sarduy, and Lezama Lima. In Spain, he became the precursor of the best poets of the early twentieth century, from García Lorca to Luis Cernuda. Perhaps, in the brilliant translation of Edith Grossman, he might have a similar effect. Read today in this new version, Góngora's masterpiece may remind English-language writers of the new millennium that, whatever their new subjects and preoccupations, their craft is still one of words, in all their astonishing, intricate, illuminating, and artificial complexity.

ALBERTO MANGUEL

NOTES

1. Luis de Góngora y Argote, *Obras en verso del Homero español que recogió Juan López de Vicuña* (1627), quoted in Dámaso Alonso, ed., *Luis de Góngora, Las Soledades* (Madrid: Revista de Occidente, 1927).
2. Juan de Jáuregui, *Antídoto contra la pestilente poesía de las "Soledades"* (1614), in Eunice J. Gates, *Documentos gongorinos* (Mexico City: El Colegio de México, 1960).
3. The reception of Góngora has been carefully analyzed in Joaquín Roses, *Góngora: Soledades habitadas* (Málaga: Universidad de Málaga, Collección Thelma, 2007).
4. Last tercets of the sonnet "De la brevedad engañosa de la vida," in Luis de Góngora, *Obra completa*, vol. 1 (Madrid: Fundación José Antonio de Castro, 2000), p. 584.
5. Benito Pérez Galdós, *Doña Perfecta* (Madrid: Alianza Editorial, Biblioteca Pérez Galdós, 1983).
6. Severo Sarduy, "El barroco y el neobarroco," in César Fernández Moreno, ed., *América latina en su literatura* (Mexico City: Unesco, 1972).
7. Bishop Sprat, *History of the Royal Society of London*, quoted in Northrop Frye, *The Harper Handbook of Literature* (New York: Harper and Row, 1985), p. 350.
8. William Shakespeare, *Richard II*, 5.2.46, in *The Oxford Shakespeare: Complete Works*, W. J. Craig (ed.) (London: Oxford University Press, 1969).
9. Jorge Luis Borges, "Sir Thomas Browne," in *Inquisiciones* (Buenos Aires: Proa, 1925), pp. 33–41.
10. Borges, "Menoscabo y grandeza de Quevedo," in *Inquisiciones* (Buenos Aires: Proa, 1925), pp. 43–49.
11. Robert Jammes, *Etudes sur l'oeuvre poétique de Don Luis de Góngora* (Bordeaux: Féret éditeur, Bibliotèque de la l'Ecole des hautes études hispaniques, 1967).
12. Díaz de Rivas, *Discursos apologéticos por el estylo del "Poliphemo" y "Soledades,"* in Eunice J. Gates, *Documentos gongorinos* (Mexico City: El Colegio de México), pp. 51–52.
13. Francisco de Córdoba, *Exámen del "Antídoto" o apología por las "Soledades,"* in M. Artigas, *Don Luis de Góngora y Argote* (Madrid: Revista de Archivos, 1925), p. 406.
14. Charles Baudelaire, "L'étranger," in *Le spleen de Paris* (1864), in *Oeuvres complètes*, vol. 1 (Paris: Gallimard, Bibliothéque de la Pléiade, 1975).
15. Jorge Luis Borges, "El Ulises de Joyce," in *Inquisiciones* (Buenos Aires: Proa, 1925), pp. 22–23.

Suggestions for Further Reading

The best edition in Spanish of the *Soledades* is that edited by Robert Jammes (Madrid: Castalia, 1994).

Further Reading in English

- Collins, Marsha S. *The Soledades, Góngora's Mask of the Imagination*. Columbia and London: University of Missouri Press, 2002.

- García Lorca, Federico. "The Poetic Image in Don Luis de Góngora." Translated by Ben Belitt. Edited by T. Weiss and Renée Weiss. *Quarterly Review of Literature: Thirtieth Anniversary Criticism Retrospective* XX (1977): 189–193.

- Jones, Royston O. "The Poetic Unity of the Soledades of Góngora." *Bulletin of Hispanic Studies* XXXI (1954): 189–204.

- Wardopper, Bruce. "The Complexity of the Simple in Góngora's Soledad primera." *The Journal of Medieval and Renaissance Studies* 7 (1977): 35–51.

- Woods, M. J. *The Poet and the Natural World in the Age of Góngora*. Oxford: Oxford University Press, 1978.

Further Reading in Spanish

- Alonso, Dámaso, ed. *Luis de Góngora: Soledades, Revista de Occidente.* Madrid, 1927.

- Borges, Jorge Luis. "Gongorismo" (1927). In *Textos Recobrados 1919–1929.* Buenos Aires: Emecé, 1997.

- Lida de Malkiel, María Rosa. "El hilo narrativo de las Soledades." *Boletín de la Academia Argentina de Letras* XXVI (1961): 349–59.

- Orozco, Emilio. *Introducción a Góngora.* Barcelona: Crítica, 1984.

- Roses, Joaquín. *Góngora: Soledades habitadas.* Málaga: Universidad de Málaga, 2007.

The Solitudes

DEDICATORIA

AL DUQUE DE BEJAR

Pasos de un peregrino son errante
cuantos me dictó versos dulce musa:
   en soledad confusa
perdidos unos, otros inspirados.

¡Oh tú, que, de venablos impedido
—muros de abeto, almenas de diamante—,
bates los montes, que, de nieve armados,
gigantes de cristal los teme el cielo;
donde el cuerno, del eco repetido,
fieras te expone, que—al teñido suelo,
muertas, pidiendo términos disformes—
espumoso coral le dan al Tormes!:

arrima a un fresno el fresno—cuyo acero,
sangre sudando, en tiempo hará breve
   purpurear la nieve—
y, en cuanto da el solícito montero
al duro robre, al pino levantado
—émulos vividores de las peñas—
   las formidables señas
del oso que aun besaba, atravesado,

DEDICATION

TO THE DUKE OF BEJAR

Steps of a wandering pilgrim are these,
the verses my sweet muse dictated to me:
   in perplexing solitude
some lost, yet others enlivened and inspired.

Oh you who, encircled by spears and lances
—ramparts of fir, battlements of diamond—
defeat the mountains that, armored in snow,
are feared now as crystal Titans[1] by heaven;
where the hunting horn, echoing, repeating,
reveals beasts to you that—on the stained earth   10
fallen dead, pleading for misshaped boundaries—
offer foaming coral to the Tormes:[2]

lean against an ash your ash—its iron,
perspiring blood, in a short while will tinge
   the snow a purple hue—
and, as the scrupulous hunter presents
to the resilient oak, the lofty pine
—living emulators of the mountain peaks—
   formidable tokens
of the bear still kissing, run through, the shaft   20

1 The gods who were the children of Uranus and Gaia and overthrew their
father under the leadership of Cronus, overthrown in turn by their children,
led by Jupiter. 2 A river in Spain.

la asta de tu luciente jabalina,
—o lo sagrado supla de la encina
lo augusto del dosel; o de la fuente
la alta zanefa, lo majestuoso
del sitïal a tu deidad debido—,
    ¡oh Duque esclarecido!,
templa en sus ondas tu fatiga ardiente,
y, entregados tus miembros al reposo
sobre el de grama césped no desnudo,
déjate un rato hallar del pie acertado
que sus errantes pasos ha votado
a la real cadena de tu escudo.

Honre süave, generoso nudo
libertad, de fortuna perseguida:
que, a tu piedad Euterpe agradecida,
su canoro dará dulce instrumento,
cuando la Fama no su trompa al viento.

of your gleaming javelin
—either allow the sacred nature of oak
to serve as an august canopy, or the fountain's
high edge to serve as majestic dignity
of the raised throne due to your excellence—
oh illustrious Duke!
temper in its flow your ardent fatigue,
and give your limbs up to the soft repose
of turf in no way bare of thick-grown grass,
for a brief time let yourself be found by the   30
unerring foot that has pledged its errant steps
to the royal chain, adornment of your shield.

Let the easy, generous loop pay honor
to liberty, persecuted by fate:
and a grateful Euterpe[1] will to your
mercy play her sonorous instrument sweet,
when Fame silences her trumpet, in the breeze.

---

1 The Muse of lyric poetry; the nine Muses were deities of the arts and sciences.

SOLEDAD
PRIMERA

Era del año la estación florida
en que el mentido robador de Europa
—media luna las armas de su frente,
y el Sol todos los rayos de su pelo—,
    luciente honor del cielo,
en campos de zafiro pace estrellas;
cuando el que ministrar podía la copa
a Júpiter mejor que el garzón de Ida,
—náufrago y desdeñado, sobre ausente—
lagrimosas de amor dulces querellas
    da al mar; que condolido,
    fué a las ondas, fué al viento
    el mísero gemido,
segundo de Arión dulce instrumento.

Del siempre en la montaña opuesto pino
    al enemigo Noto,
    piadoso miembro roto

THE FIRST
SOLITUDE

It was the flowering season of the year
when Europa's false-hearted abductor
—a half moon the weapons on his brow,
the Sun's rays all the strands of his hair[1]—
    oh bright glory of heaven,
grazes on stars in fields of sapphire blue;
when one who could pour the wine for Jupiter
better than the comely lad of Ida,[2]
—a shipwrecked youth, one scorned and desolate—
weeps sweet complaints of love   10
    to the sea; taking pity,
    for the waves and for the wind
    it made of his abject tears
a second sweet instrument of Arion.[3]

From a pine always struggling in the mountains
    with Notus[4] the enemy
    a merciful broken limb

---

1 Jupiter, in the form of a bull, abducted and violated Europa. Taurus (the bull) is the sign of spring (April 21–May 21), "the flowering season." 2 Ganymede of Ida was Jupiter's cupbearer. 3 The crew of the ship carrying the musician Arion from Italy to Corinth wanted to throw him overboard and take his money. He asked that they allow him to sing first; dolphins gathered at the sound, and Arion escaped the sailors by plunging into the sea. He was rescued by a dolphin that carried him to land on its back. 4 The south or southwestern wind, called Auster by the Romans.

—breve tabla—delfín no fué pequeño
al inconsiderado peregrino
20   que a una Libia de ondas su camino
    fió, y su vida a un leño.

Del Océano pues antes sorbido,
    y luego vomitado
no lejos de un escollo coronado
de secos juncos, de calientes plumas,
    —alga todo y espumas—
halló hospitalidad donde halló nido
    de Júpiter el ave.

Besa la arena, y de la rota nave
30   aquella parte poca
que le expuso en la playa dió a la roca:
    que aun se dejan las peñas
lisonjear de agradecidas señas.

Desnudo el joven, cuanto ya el vestido
    Océano ha bebido,
restituir le hace a las arenas;
    y al sol lo extiende luego,
    que, lamiéndolo apenas
su dulce lengua de templado fuego,
40   lento lo embiste, y con süave estilo
la menor onda chupa al menor hilo.

No bien pues de su luz los horizontes
—que hacían desigual, confusamente
montes de agua y piélagos de montes—
    desdorados los siente,
cuando—entregado el mísero extranjero
en lo que ya del mar redimió fiero—

—mere slender plank—was not too small a dolphin
for the thoughtless wanderer, a pilgrim
entrusting his path to a Libya of waves,   20
    his life to a scrap of wood.[1]

By Ocean first gulped down, by Ocean swallowed
    and then vomited, spat out
not far from a reef rising from the sea,
crowned with dry reeds and rushes, still warm feathers
    —all seaweed and ocean spume—
he found refuge in the place where Jupiter's
    favored raptor[2] built a nest.

He kisses the sand, and from the shattered ship
    the spare and meager fragment   30
that brought him to the beach he offers the rocks:
    even crags confess themselves
flattered by signs and shows of gratitude.

The young man strips, and all that his apparel
    had drunk of Ocean's water
he causes to be returned to the reef's sand;
    he spreads the clothes in the sun,
    which, barely licking at them
with its soft tongue of moderating fire,
sets upon them slowly, and in gentle fashion   40
sucks the smallest ripple from the smallest thread.

Then as soon as he perceives horizons
    —that changeably, confusedly became
mountains of water, open seas of mountains—
    losing their golden hue,
    —the wretched stranger once again embraced
what he had rescued from the savage sea—

1 Libya is often used as a synonym for the desert. The plank is compared to
the dolphin that rescued Arion. 2 The eagle is the bird sacred to Jupiter.

entre espinas crepúsculos pisando,
riscos que aun igualara mal, volando,
    veloz, intrépida ala,
—menos cansado que confuso—escala.

    Vencida al fin la cumbre
    —del mar siempre sonante,
    de la muda campaña
árbitro igual e inexpugnable muro—,
    con pie ya más seguro
    declina al vacilante
breve esplendor de mal distinta lumbre:
    farol de una cabaña
que sobre el ferro está, en aquel incierto
golfo de sombras anunciando el puerto.

    «Rayos—les dice—ya que no de Leda
trémulos hijos, sed de mi fortuna
término luminoso.» Y—recelando
de invidïosa bárbara arboleda
    interposición, cuando
de vientos no conjuración alguna—
    cual, haciendo el villano
la fragosa montaña fácil llano,
    atento sigue aquella
—aun a pesar de las tinieblas bella,
aun a pesar de las estrellas clara—
    piedra, indigna tiara
—si tradición apócrifa no miente—
de animal tenebroso, cuya frente
carro es brillante de nocturno día:
    tal, diligente, el paso
    el joven apresura,

and scraping through gashing brambles barbed and thorned
on cliffs dusk-tinged, barely yielding to the flight
   of agile, intrepid wings   50
—less weary than awestruck—the young man scales them.

   Vanquishing at last the peak
   —to the always sounding sea
   and countryside ever mute
the neutral judge and wall impregnable—
   now with more certain step
   he descends to the vacillant
brief gleam of a distant, an indistinct light:
   a beacon in a cabin
lying at anchor amid the hazards of   60
a dark gulf of shadows to announce the port.

"Beams"—he calls—"if not the light of Leda's
glistering sons,[1] then be to my ill fortune
a luminous conclusion." And—fearful of
the envy of uncultivated trees
   interposing between, or
any kind of conspiracy of winds—
   moving like a rustic who
turns the overgrown slope into easy plain,
   attentive he pursues the   70
—even in spite of darkness beautiful,
even in spite of starlight radiant—
   gem,[2] undeserved coronet
—if apocryphal tradition does not lie—
of a tenebrous gloom-loving beast, whose brow
the brilliant carriage is of nocturnal day:
   like that, diligent, the lad
   hastens and speeds his pace,

1 Castor and Pollux, also called the Dioscuri. Their sister was Helen. They
were placed in the heavens as the Gemini. 2 According to a medieval tradi-
tion, the carbuncle was worn on the forehead of the tiger (and sometimes the
stag) and functioned as a lantern at night.

midiendo la espesura
80 con igual pie que el raso,
fijo—a despecho de la niebla fría—
en el carbunclo, norte de su aguja,
o el Austro brame o la arboleda cruja.

El can ya, vigilante,
convoca, despidiendo al caminante;
    y la que desviada
luz poca pareció, tanta es vecina,
que yace en ella la robusta encina,
mariposa en cenizas desatada.

90 Llegó pues el mancebo, y saludado,
sin ambición, sin pompa de palabras,
de los conducidores fué de cabras,
que a Vulcano tenían coronado.

    ¡Oh bienaventurado
    albergue a cualquier hora,
templo de Pales, alquería de Flora!
    No moderno artificio
borró designios, bosquejó modelos,
al cóncavo ajustando de los cielos
100   el sublime edificio;
    retamas sobre robre
    tu fábrica son pobre,
    do guarda, en vez de acero,
    la inocencia al cabrero
    más que el silbo al ganado.
    ¡Oh bienaventurado
    albergue a cualquier hora!

measuring the undergrowth
with the same step as clear ground,   80
fixed—in defiance of cold misty fog—
on the carbuncle, polestar to his compass,
though Austral wind[1] roar or woodlands creak and groan.

Canis[2] now, vigilant,
calls out, bidding the walker leave, depart;
    and light that seemed so far
and so small is now so near and now so great
that a mighty, robust oak lies within,
a butterfly that crumbles into ashes.

And so the youth drew close, and he was greeted   90
plainly, with no ceremonious words,
by simple herders and drivers of goats
who on the brow of Vulcan[3] had placed a crown.

Oh fortunate, oh happy
    shelter at any hour,
temple of Pales, Flora's sanctuary![4]
    No modern artifice
corrected your designs, sketched out your models,
adapting to concavities of sky
    your edifice sublime;   100
    branches of broom on oak
    are your entire construction,
    where in lieu of the sword
    innocence guards the goatherd
better than a whistle protects the flock.
    Oh fortunate, oh happy
    shelter at any hour!

1 The south or southwest wind (i.e., Auster). 2 Canis is Latin for dog.
3 The Roman god of fire. 4 Pales is the Roman god (or goddess) of shep-
herds, Flora the goddess of flowers.

No en ti la ambición mora
hidrópica de viento,
110   ni la que su alimento
el áspid es gitano;
no la que, en vulto comenzando humano,
acaba en mortal fiera,
esfinge bachillera,
que hace hoy a Narciso
ecos solicitar, desdeñar fuentes;
ni la que en salvas gasta impertinentes
la pólvora del tiempo más preciso:
ceremonia profana
120   que la sinceridad burla villana
sobre el corvo cayado.
¡Oh bienaventurado
albergue a cualquier hora!

Tus umbrales ignora
la adulación, sirena
de reales palacios, cuya arena
besó ya tanto, leño:
trofeos dulces de un canoro sueño.
No a la soberbia está aquí la mentira
130   dorándole los pies, en cuanto gira
la esfera de sus plumas,
ni de los rayos baja a las espumas
favor de cera alado.

In you does not dwell the
thirsting desire of vanity,
nor one whose sustenance   *110*
is the Egyptian asp;[1]
nor one that begins with a human face
and ends as a savage beast,[2]
a prating garrulous sphinx,
that makes Narcissus today
woo echoes and display disdain for fountains;[3]
nor one who wastes in volleys presumptuous
the powder of an indispensable time:[4]
    irreverent ceremony
that a rustic sincerity derides   *120*
    over the crook of a staff.
    Oh fortunate, oh happy
    shelter at any hour!

    Your thresholds do not know
    adulation, the siren
of royal palaces, whose sands already
    have been kissed by so much wood:
sweetest trophies of melodious dreams.[5]
And falsehood is not here, gilding the feet
of vanity while it fans out and opens   *130*
    its feathered sphere of plumage,[6]
nor does favor winged in wax fall away
    from flames, plunging into waves.[7]

---

1 Envy feeds on the venom of the asp. 2 Dissimulation is the probable
allusion. 3 Narcissus fell in love with his own reflection, ignoring the love
of the nymph Echo, and eventually was transformed into the flower that
bears his name. 4 The reference is to the etiquette and protocols of the
court. 5 The image extends the reference to the siren (the mythical crea-
ture who lures sailors to their deaths) by referring to the wood of ships
wrecked on the sands (that is, deceived courtiers brought to ruin), lulled by
the siren's song. 6 The peacock, despite its beautiful plumage, has ugly
feet that are overlooked by falsehood. 7 Icarus made wings held together
by wax but flew too near the sun, fell into the sea, and was drowned.

¡Oh bienaventurado
albergue a cualquier hora!

No pues de aquella sierra—engendradora
más de fierezas que de cortesía—
   la gente parecía
   que hospedó al forastero
con pecho igual de aquel candor primero,
   que, en las selvas contento,
tienda el fresno le dió, el robre alimento.

Limpio sayal, en vez de blanco lino,
   cubrió el cuadrado pino;
y en boj, aunque rebelde, a quien el torno
forma elegante dió sin culto adorno,
leche que exprimir vió la Alba aquel día
   —mientras perdían con ella
los blancos lilios de su frente bella—,
   gruesa le dan y fría,
impenetrable casi a la cuchara,
del viejo Alcimedón invención rara.

El que de cabras fué dos veces ciento
esposo casi un lustro—cuyo diente
no perdonó a racimo aun en la frente
de Baco, cuanto más en su sarmiento—
(triunfador siempre de celosas lides,
lo coronó el Amor; mas rival tierno,
breve de barba y duro no de cuerno,
redimió con su muerte tantas vides)
   servido ya en cecina,
purpúreos hilos es de grana fina.

Sobre corchos después, más regalado
sueño le solicitan pieles blandas,

Oh fortunate, oh happy
shelter at any hour!

Not from those mountainous ranges—birthplace
to savage beasts more than to courtesy—
    did the goat herders seem
    who welcomed in the stranger
with a heart like that of our first innocence,   *140*
    when, content in the forests,
the ash tree gave us shelter, the oak our food.

A length of clean coarse wool, and not white linen,
    covered the square pine plank;
and in boxwood, though unyielding, to which
a lathe had given elegant form with no
refined adornment, milk the Dawn that day saw
    drawn—to which white lilies worn
round her beautiful brow could not compare—,
    they give to him, thick and cold,   *150*
almost impenetrable to the spoon,
that rare device of ancient Alcimedon.[1]

He who of twice one hundred she-goats had been
the consort for close to a lustrum—whose tooth
forgave no cluster even on the brow
of Bacchus, and never on his grapevine[2]—
(constant victor in battles with opponents
he was crowned by Love; but a young rival,
sparse of beard and even ductile of horn,
redeemed with his elder's death uncounted vines)   *160*
    now is served as cured dried meat,
the purple-hued threads of fine scarlet cloth.

Afterward on cork bark, a deeper, more pleasant
sleep courted by skins both soft and deep than

1 An exceptional woodcarver mentioned by Virgil in one of his eclogues. 2 Bacchus was the god of wine, winemaking, and cultivation of the grape.

que al príncipe entre holandas,
púrpura tiria o milanés brocado.
No de humosos vinos agravado
es Sísifo en la cuesta, si en la cumbre
de ponderosa vana pesadumbre,
170   es, cuanto más despierto, más burlado.
De trompa militar no, o destemplado
son de cajas, fué el sueño interrumpido;
    de can sí, embravecido
    contra la seca hoja
que el viento repeló a alguna coscoja.

Durmió, y recuerda al fin, cuando las aves
—esquilas dulces de sonora pluma—
    señas dieron süaves
del alba al Sol, que el pabellón de espuma
180   dejó, y en su carroza
rayó el verde obelisco de la choza.

Agradecido, pues, el peregrino,
deja el albergue y sale acompañado
de quien lo lleva donde, levantado,
distante pocos pasos del camino,
imperioso mira la campaña
un escollo, apacible galería,
que festivo teatro fué algún día
de cuantos pisan faunos la montaña.

190   Llegó, y, a vista tanta
obedeciendo la dudosa planta,
inmóvil se quedó sobre un lentisco,
verde balcón del agradable risco.

is granted to a prince 'tween Holland sheets,
Tyrian purple or Milanese brocade.
Not by aged smoky wines weighed down is he,
no Sisyphus[1] on the slope of the mountain
where at the top by heavy haughty grief
he is, the more he wakes, the more derided.   *170*
Not by military horn nor dissonant
clang of moneyboxes his sleep disturbed;
    but by canis, yes, raging
    against the dead withered leaf
torn by the wind from a nearby kermes oak.

He slept and awakes at last when the birds
—sweet tiny bells of melodious feathers—
    rang out a tender signal
of dawn to the Sun, who rose from his couch of
    foam, and from his chariot   *180*
shone rays on the green obelisk of the hut.

And so, filled with gratitude, the pilgrim
leaves the refuge and goes out accompanied
by one who leads him to the place where, lofty,
distant but a few paces from the path,
imperious, gazing at the countryside,
rises a ridge, peaceable gallery
that long ago a rollicking theater was
for every faun[2] that once dwelled on the mountain.

There he arrived, and his hesitant foot,   *190*
obedient to the sight of that expanse,
remained unmoving on a mastic tree,
green balcony to the pleasant crest of reef.

---

1 Punished by the gods, Sisyphus was condemned to eternally roll a heavy
boulder up a hill only to have it roll down again as soon as he reached the
top.   2 A deity comparable to a satyr and identified with Pan, with a goat's
horns and feet.

Si mucho poco mapa les despliega,
mucho es más lo que, nieblas desatando,
confunde el sol y la distancia niega.
Muda la admiración, habla callando,
y, ciega, un río sigue, que—luciente
    de aquellos montes hijo—
con torcido discurso, aunque prolijo,
tiraniza los campos útilmente;
orladas sus orillas de frutales,
quiere la Copia que su cuerno sea
—si al animal armaron de Amaltea
    diáfanos cristales—;
engazando edificios en su plata,
    de muros se corona,
rocas abraza, islas aprisiona,
de la alta gruta donde se desata
hasta los jaspes líquidos, adonde
su orgullo pierde y su memoria esconde.

«Aquéllas que los árboles apenas
dejan ser torres hoy—dijo el cabrero
con muestras de dolor extraordinarias—
las estrellas nocturnas luminarias
    eran de sus almenas,
cuando el que ves sayal fué limpio acero.
Yacen ahora, y sus desnudas piedras
    visten piadosas yedras:
    que a rüinas y a estragos,
sabe el tiempo hacer verdes halagos.»

Con gusto el joven y atención le oía,
cuando torrente de armas y de perros,
que si precipitados no los cerros,
las personas tras de un lobo traía,
tierno discurso y dulce compañía

If this small map unfolds so much to them,
much more, clouds of mist lifting, lies beyond,
confounded by sun and by distance denied.
Wonder is mute, it speaks by being silent,
and, blind, it follows a river, that—shining
    child of those precipices—
in convoluted discourse, and digressive,   *200*
benevolent it tyrannizes the fields;
with its banks ornamented by fruit trees,
Copia¹ herself desires it for her horn
—if the creature of Amalthea² had been armed
    with crystal transparency—;
setting edifices in its silver,
    crowning itself with walls,
it embraces rocks, imprisons islands,
from the high grotto where it first breaks free
to the opaque jasper waters deep where   *210*
pride is lost and memory hides away.

"Today the trees almost completely hide
    those towers"—said the goatherd
with extraordinary signs of sorrow—
"but yesterday the stars, nocturnal lights,
    shone in their battlements,
when one you see here in wool wore speckless metal.
They have fallen now, and their naked stones
    are dressed in merciful ivy:
    for ruins and devastation   *220*
time knows how to flatter and grace with green."

With attentive pleasure the young man listened,
when a torrent of weapons and of dogs,
as if not plunging down the mountains themselves,
brought a party of hunters after a wolf,
all gentle discourse and sweet company

---

1 The goddess of plenty; her horn is the cornucopia.   2 The goat that suckled Zeus (Jupiter). Her horn was the one used by Copia.

dejar hizo al serrano,
que—del sublime espacïoso llano
al huésped al camino reduciendo—
230 al venatorio estruendo,
 pasos dando veloces,
número crece y multiplica voces.

Bajaba entre sí el joven admirando,
armado a Pan o semicapro a Marte,
en el pastor mentidos, que con arte
culto principio dió al discurso, cuando
rémora de sus pasos fué su oído,
 dulcemente impedido
de canoro instrumento, que pulsado
240 era de una serrana junto a un tronco,
sobre un arroyo, de quejarse ronco,
mudo sus ondas, cuando no enfrenado.

Otra con ella montaraz zagala
juntaba el cristal líquido al humano
por el arcaduz bello de una mano
que al uno menosprecia, al otro iguala.

Del verde margen otra las mejores
rosas traslada y lilios al cabello,
o por lo matizado o por lo bello,
250 si Aurora no con rayos, Sol con flores.

Negras pizarras entre blancos dedos
ingenïosa hiere otra, que dudo
que aun los peñascos la escucharan quedos.
 Al son pues deste rudo

making the goatherd forsake,
and—from the sublime and spacious clearing
leading his guest back again to the path—
    to the clamorous hunt   230
    racing with light-footed speed
he increases their number and swells their shouts.

Filled with amazement the young man descended,
fully armed Pan or semicaprine Mars[1]
the shepherd seemed to him, with art so learned
had he given commencement to the discourse,
when his ear became a hindrance to his steps,
    so sweetly impeded
by a melodious instrument strummed
by a mountain girl sitting under a tree,   240
beside a stream, made hoarse by its complaining
    rills, mute now if not restrained.

With her another lass of the countryside
joined liquid crystal to the human kind
by the beautiful conduit of a hand
that scorns the one, is equal to the other.[2]

From the green verge another girl removes
the best roses and lilies to her hair,
and with the blend of color or her beauty,
if not Aurora with rays, Sun with flowers.[3]   250

Pieces of black slate between white fingers
another, ingenious, strikes, so that I doubt
even the crags can hear her and be still.
    To the sound, then, of this crude

1 Pan, the rustic god with goat's horns and hooves, and Mars, the god of war, seem to share attributes as they merge in the figure of the shepherd.   2 The image evokes the girl using her hand to bring water to her face (for washing or drinking).   3 Again, Góngora exchanges the attributes of mythological figures; flowers are associated with Aurora (dawn), rays with the Sun.

sonoroso instrumento
—lasciva el movimiento,
mas los ojos honesta—
altera otra, bailando, la floresta.

Tantas al fin el arroyuelo, y tantas
montañesas da el prado, que dirías
ser menos las que verdes Hamadrías
abortaron las plantas:
inundación hermosa
que la montaña hizo populosa
de sus aldeas todas
a pastorales bodas.

De una encina embebido
en lo cóncavo, el joven mantenía
la vista de hermosura, y el oído
de métrica armonía.
El sileno buscaba
de aquellas que la sierra dió bacantes
—ya que ninfas las niega ser errantes
el hombro sin aljaba—;
o si—del Termodonte
émulo el arroyuelo desatado
de aquel fragoso monte—
escuadrón de amazonas, desarmado,
tremola en sus riberas
pacíficas banderas.

Vulgo lascivo erraba
—al voto del mancebo,
el yugo de ambos sexos sacudido—

and sonorous instrument
—lascivious the movement,
  but modesty in her eyes—
another disquiets, dancing, the greensward.

So many girls at the brook, simply so many
mountain girls in the meadow, you would say   260
the green Hamadryades[1] were fewer, the ones
  who live and die with their trees:
  a most beautiful deluge
that the populous mountain sent flowing
  from all its tiny hamlets
  to a rustic wedding feast.

  Thunderstruck in the hollow
of an oak, the young man kept and maintained
his eyes fixed on the beauty and his ears
  on the metered harmony.   270
  He searched for the Silenus[2]
of those Bacchantes[3] that the mountain offered
—since errant nymphs they cannot be because
  their shoulders bear no quiver—;
  nor—unless of the Thermodon[4]
the competitor is the brook unleashed
  by that clamorous mountain—
a squadron of Amazons,[5] unweaponed,
  fluttering on its banks
  banners and pennants of peace.   280

  Antic mountain lads wandered
  —to the mind of the young man
the yoke that links both sexes shaken off—

---

1 The nymphs associated with trees. 2 An older satyr, the constant companion of Bacchus. 3 Female companions of Bacchus. 4 The river where the capital of the Amazons was located. 5 A race of warrior women.

al tiempo que—de flores impedido
  el que ya serenaba
la región de su frente rayo nuevo—
purpúrea terneruela, conducida
de su madre, no menos enramada,
entre albogues se ofrece, acompañada
  de juventud florida.

Cuál dellos las pendientes sumas graves
de negras baja, de crestadas aves,
cuyo lascivo esposo vigilante
doméstico es del Sol nuncio canoro,
y—de coral barbado—no de oro
ciñe, sino de púrpura, turbante.

  Quién la cerviz oprime
  con la manchada copia
de los cabritos más retozadores,
  tan golosos, que gime
el que menos peinar puede las flores
  de su guirnalda propia.

  No el sitio, no, fragoso,
no el torcido taladro de la tierra,
  privilegió en la sierra
la paz del conejuelo temeroso;
trofeo ya su número es a un hombro,
  si carga no y asombro.

  Tú, ave peregrina,
arrogante esplendor—ya que no bello—
  del último Occidente:
penda el rugoso nácar de tu frente
sobre el crespo zafiro de tu cuello,
que Himeneo a sus mesas te destina.

at the same time that—by flowers surrounded
  the budding beams that now
began to grace the region of her brow—
a radiant calf, a heifer, guided by
her mother, no less adorned with blossoms,
among the flageolets appears, along
  with youths bedecked by blooms.   290

One of them descends the slopes, in his hands
weighty masses of black and crested hens,
their lusty consort, the domicile's guardian,
is to the Sun a musical nuncio,
and—bearded in coral—has girded on a
headdress not of gold but of purple hue.

  Another burdens his neck
  with the spotted semblances
of the most capricious of young caprine bucks,
  so gluttonous that the one   300
howls who cannot rake over the flowers
  of his own crowning wreath.

  Not the rugged setting, no,
and not the twisted burrow in the earth,
  could favor in the mountains
the peace of the fearful rabbit, tremulous;
their great numbers a trophy on a shoulder,
  no burden this, but wonder.

  You, oh singular bird,
arrogant splendor—for it is not comely—   310
  of the remote Occident:[1]
hang the wrinkled nacre of your forehead
down over the kinked sapphire of your neck,
for Hymeneus[2] wants you on his tables.

---

1 The turkey, native to the New World. 2 Also called Hymen, he is the
god of weddings.

Sobre dos hombros larga vara ostenta
en cien aves cien picos de rubíes,
tafiletes calzadas carmesíes,
 emulación y afrenta
 aun de los berberiscos,
320 en la inculta región de aquellos riscos.

Lo que lloró la Aurora
 —si es néctar lo que llora—,
y, antes que el Sol, enjuga
la abeja que madruga
a libar flores y a chupar cristales,
en celdas de oro líquido, en panales
 la orza contenía
 que un montañés traía.

No excedía la oreja
330 el pululante ramo
 del ternezuelo gamo,
 que mal llevar se deja,
y con razón: que el tálamo desdeña
la sombra aun de lisonja tan pequeña.

El arco del camino pues torcido,
 —que habían con trabajo
por la fragosa cuerda del atajo
las gallardas serranas desmentido—
de la cansada juventud vencido,
340 —los fuertes hombros con las cargas graves,
 treguas hechas süaves—
sueño le ofrece a quien buscó descanso
el ya sañudo arroyo, ahora manso:

Across two backs a long staff makes display
of one hundred ruby beaks, one hundred birds,
scarlet slippers in Moroccan leather,[1]
　　emulation and challenge
　　even to those of Berbers
in the untilled region of the cliffs and crags.　　　　　*320*

　　Liquor that Aurora wept
　　—if nectar is what she weeps—
　　before the Sun, is dried
　　by the bee, early riser
to sip at flowers and drink crystal drops,
in cells of liquid gold, in honeycombs
　　contained in the gallipot
　　carried by a mountain lad.

　　No longer than an ear
　　the sprouting shoot in bud　　　　　*330*
　　of the very young bull calf,
　　struggling against being borne,
and with reason: for the nuptial bed disdains
even the shadow of such small flattery.[2]

The bent and tortuous bow of the road
　　—which so laboriously
the beautiful mountain girls had challenged
along the brambled shortcut of the cord[3]—
conquered at last by the wearied youths,
—the strong men with their weighty burdens　　　　　*340*
　　declaring a gentle truce—
sleep offered to any who searched for rest
by the once raging stream, now pacified:

1 The description is of partridges with red beaks, and red legs compared to
the slippers of Berbers.　2 The calf is just growing horns, which are a symbol
of cuckoldry, and therefore disdained by the "nuptial bed."　3 The girls had
followed the straighter but more difficult path—the string of the bow—while
the boys, carrying their burdens, took the longer but easier one.

merced de la hermosura que ha hospedado,
efectos, si no, dulces, del concento
que, en las lucientes de marfil clavijas,
las duras cuerdas de las negras guijas
hicieron a su curso acelerado,
en cuanto a su furor perdonó el viento.

350   Menos en renunciar tardó la encina
        el extranjero errante,
que en reclinarse el menos fatigado
sobre la grana que se viste fina,
su bella amada, deponiendo amante
en las vestidas rosas su cuidado.

Saludólos a todos cortésmente,
        y—admirado no menos
de los serranos que correspondido—
las sombras solicita de unas peñas.
360   De lágrimas los tiernos ojos llenos,
reconociendo el mar en el vestido
—que beberse no pudo el Sol ardiente
las que siempre dará cerúleas señas—
        político serrano,
de canas grave, habló desta manera:

        «¿Cuál tigre, la más fiera
        que clima infamó hircano,
        dió el primer alimento
al que—ya deste o aquel mar—primero
370   surcó, labrador fiero,
el campo undoso en mal nacido pino,
        vaga Clicie del viento,

thanks to the great beauty it has harbored,
or perhaps sweet effects of the harmony
that, in the gleaming slim pegs of marble,[1]
the harsh chords of smooth black pebbles
had on the rush of its hurrying current,
when the wind absolved it from its fury.

In less time than it took the errant stranger   *350*
    to renounce the trunk of oak,
the least weary of the loving mountain lads
reclined on cloth of finest scarlet worn
by his beautiful love, the lover laying aside
on roseate skirts his trouble and his care.

He greeted all of them with courtesy,
    and—the mountain girls and men
no less amazed than responsive to his words—
solicits the shade cast by cliffs and crags.
    Tender eyes filling with tears,   *360*
recognizing the sea in his apparel
—for the ardent Sun could not drink up all
the cerulean traces it will always leave—
    tactful and discreet, one man
grave with his white hair, spoke in this manner:

    "Did a tiger, the fiercest
    that ravaged Hyrcania,[2]
    give suck, our first food, to one
—whether in this or another sea—who first
    plowed, a savage farmer,   *370*
the undulant field in a luckless pine,[3]
    vague Clytie[4] to the wind,

1 The image evokes, in the guise of an instrument, the girls' music described earlier. 2 A province of the Persian Empire, located on the Caspian Sea. 3 Góngora compares the ocean to an "undulant field." The "savage farmer" is the mariner in a "luckless pine," or ship. 4 A nymph disdained by Apollo and transformed by the gods into a heliotrope, a flower that follows the sun.

en telas hecho—antes que en flor—el lino?
Más armas introdujo este marino
monstruo, escamado de robustas hayas,
a las que tanto mar divide playas,
    que confusión y fuego
al frigio muro el otro leño griego.

Náutica industria investigó tal piedra,
    que, cual abraza yedra
escollo, el metal ella fulminante
de que Marte se viste, y, lisonjera,
solicita el que más brilla diamante
en la nocturna capa de la esfera,
estrella a nuestro polo más vecina;
    y, con virtud no poca,
    distante la revoca,
    elevada la inclina
    ya de la Aurora bella
al rosado balcón, ya a la que sella
    cerúlea tumba fría
    las cenizas del día.

En esta, pues, fiándose, atractiva,
del Norte amante dura, alado roble,
no hay tormentoso cabo que no doble,
ni isla hoy a su vuelo fugitiva.
Tifis el primer leño mal seguro
condujo, muchos luego Palinuro;
si bien por un mar ambos, que la tierra
    estanque dejó hecho,

380

390

400

canvas turned into—not a flower—but sails?
More weapons were introduced by this marine
monster, covered in scales of stalwart beech,
to strands separated by so much sea,
    than confusion and fire
by another Greek bark to the Phrygian wall.[1]

Nautical industry explored this rare stone[2]
    that, as ivy embraces   380
the reef, grasps at the fulminating metal
that Mars puts on and wears and, a flatterer,
it woos the diamond that most brilliant shines
in the nocturnal mantle of the orb,
the star most proximate to our northern pole;
    and, with strength and potency
    repels when it nearby
    is risen, and then inclines
    either to the rosy hued
balcony of fair Aurora, or to one   390
    who seals ashes of the day
    in cold cerulean tomb.[3]

Trusting, then, the winged oak, in this, attractive,
    hard lover of the North,[4]
there is no stormy cape it cannot round,
no island that today can flee its flight.
Tiphys piloted the first bark, not secure,
then Palinurus, at the helm of many;[5]
even though both sailed a sea that the earth
    transformed into a pond,   400

---

1 The allusion is to the wooden horse, filled with men and arms, brought through the walls of Troy by the Greeks. 2 The lodestone has strong magnetic properties and was used as an early compass. 3 The western sea where the sun dies each day. 4 That is, the compass. 5 Tiphys was helmsman on the first vessel, the Argo, ship of the Argonauts; Palinurus piloted the fleet of Aeneas.

cuyo famoso estrecho
una y otra de Alcides llave cierra.

Piloto hoy la Codicia, no de errantes
árboles, mas de selvas inconstantes,
al padre de las aguas Ocëano
   —de cuya monarquía
   el Sol, que cada día
nace en sus ondas y en sus ondas muere,
los términos saber todos no quiere—
410   dejó primero de su espuma cano,
   sin admitir segundo
en inculcar sus límites al mundo.

Abetos suyos tres aquel tridente
   violaron a Neptuno,
conculcado hasta allí de otro ninguno,
besando las que al Sol el Occidente
le corre en lecho azul de aguas marinas,
   turquesadas cortinas.

A pesar luego de áspides volantes
420   —sombra del sol y tósigo del viento—
de caribes flechados, sus banderas
siempre gloriosas, siempre tremolantes,
rompieron los que armó de plumas ciento
lestrigones el istmo, aladas fieras:
el istmo que al Océano divide,

and its famed strait, enclosed,
shut in by keys of Alcides.[1]

Appetence now is pilot, not of errant
trees, but of entire, mutable forests,
and first to leave Ocean, the father of waters
   —of whose vast royal domain
   the Sun, who day after day
is born in his waves and in his waves finds death,
does not wish to know boundaries or extent—
with hair turned white by the spume greed leaves behind,   *410*
   though he admits no second
in professing those limits to the world.

Three firs of Appetence were those that violated
   the trident of Neptune,
venturing farther than any other,
kissing the turquoise curtains that Occident
closes for the Sun in his dark blue bed
   of deep marine waters.[2]

Then in spite of flying asps
   —shadow on the sun and venom on the wind—   *420*
of arrowed Caribs, greed's flags and banners
always glorious, always fluttering
broke the Lestrigons that the isthmus armed
with multitudes of feathers, beasts with wings:[3]
the isthmus that divides Ocean in two,[4]

1 Alcides is another name of Hercules; the Strait of Gibraltar, entrance to the Mediterranean (the "pond"), lies between two promontories called the Pillars of Hercules in ancient times. 2 The allusion is to the three ships of Columbus, which ventured into portions of the ocean that modern Europeans had not sailed before. 3 Lestrigons were a race of cannibalistic giants encountered by Ulysses. Góngora compares them to the Carib Indians who fought the Spaniards with ferocity. Their venom-tipped arrows are compared to flying poisonous snakes, fired in such great numbers that they dimmed the sun. 4 The Isthmus of Panama that divides the ocean as if it were a crystal snake, its head the Northern Sea (the Atlantic), its tail the Southern (the Pacific).

y—sierpe de cristal—juntar le impide
la cabeza, del Norte coronada,
con la que ilustra el Sur cola escamada
   de antárticas estrellas.

430 Segundos leños dió a segundo polo
en nuevo mar, que le rindió no sólo
las blancas hijas de sus conchas bellas,
mas los que lograr bien no supo Midas
   metales homicidas.

No le bastó después a este elemento
conducir orcas, alistar ballenas,
murarse de montañas espumosas,
infamar blanqueando sus arenas
con tantas del primer atrevimiento
440 señas—aun a los bueitres lastimosas—,
para con estas lastimosas señas
temeridades enfrenar segundas.

Tú, Codicia, tú, pues, de las profundas
estigias aguas torpe marinero,
cuantos abre sepulcros el mar fiero
   a tus huesos, desdeñas.

El promontorio que Éolo sus rocas
candados hizo de otras nuevas grutas
para el Austro de alas nunca enjutas,
450 para el Cierzo espirante por cien bocas,
doblaste alegre, y tu obstinada entena
cabo le hizo de Esperanza Buena.

and—serpent of crystal—prevents the union
    of the head, in the North crowned,
and the scaled tail that illuminates the South
    with Antarctican stars.

Greed sent second barks to a second pole   430
in a new sea that offered him not only
the beautiful white daughters of its shells,
but murderous metals Midas never learned
    to possess successfully.[1]

Then it was not enough that this element[2]
guided in orcas, enlisted monstrous whales,
erected battlements of foaming mountains,
defamed its own sands by blanching them white
with so many traces of the first daring
venture—piteous even to the vultures—   440
for those piteous traces to restrain
a second wave of bold temerities.

You, Appetence, oh you, hellish mariner
    of deep Stygian waters,[3]
you scorn all the sepulchers the savage sea
    opens wide for your bones.

The promontory whose rocks Aeolus[4] used
as locks for other new grottoes, a cave
for Auster the wind with wings that never dry,
for Mistral[5] who breathes through a hundred mouths,   450
you rounded joyfully, and with obstinate
lateen yard transformed the cape into Good Hope.

---

1 The riches of the Pacific that came to Spain: from pearls to precious metals. 2 The ocean, which attacked the navigators, sank their ships, and killed their men. 3 The River Styx (Stygian is its adjective) encircles the nether world. 4 Aeolus had control of the winds, which he kept in caves. 5 A north or northwest wind that can reach violent proportions (as if it blew through a hundred mouths).

Tantos luego astronómicos presagios
frustrados, tanta náutica doctrina,
debajo aun de la zona más vecina
al Sol, calmas vencidas y naufragios,
los reinos de la Aurora al fin besaste,
cuyos purpúreos senos perlas netas,
    cuyas minas secretas
460   hoy te guardan su más precioso engaste;
la aromática selva penetraste,
que al pájaro de Arabia—cuyo vuelo
    arco alado es del cielo,
    no corvo, mas tendido—
pira le erige, y le construye nido.

Zodíaco después fué cristalino
    a glorïoso pino,
émulo vago del ardiente coche
    del Sol, este elemento,
470   que cuatro veces había sido ciento
dosel al día y tálamo a la noche,
cuando halló de fugitiva plata
la bisagra, aunque estrecha, abrazadora
de un Océano y otro, siempre uno,
o las columnas bese o la escarlata,
    tapete de la aurora.
    Esta pues nave, ahora,
en el húmido templo de Neptuno
varada pende a la inmortal memoria
480   con nombre de Victoria.

After so many auguries in the stars
frustrated, so much doctrine of the sea,
even below the zone that closest lies
to the Sun, calms overcome, and shipwrecks,
the kingdoms of Aurora at last you kissed,[1]
whose purple bosom today guards lustrous pearls,
    whose secret hidden mines
keep for you their mountings most sumptuous;   460
you penetrated aromatic forests,
where the bird of Arabia—whose flight
    winged rainbow is in the sky,
    not curved but long, extended—
builds its funeral pyre when it builds its nest.[2]

Then this element was a crystalline
    zodiac to a pine most
glorious, errant rival to the fiery
    carriage of the ardent Sun,
and four times a hundred spans it had been   470
a canopy in the day, a bed at night,
when it discovered the hinge of fugitive
    silver embracing, although
narrow, one ocean and another, truly
one, whether kissing the pillars or the
    scarlet hanging of the dawn.[3]
    And so this vessel, now
run aground in Neptune's watery temple
    awaits immortal renown,
    bearing the name Victoria.   480

1 The East Indies, reached at last by Appetence, or Greed. 2 The phoenix, a bird that lived five hundred years, then immolated itself; a young phoenix rose from its ashes. 3 This extended image evokes the four-hundred-day voyage of the Victoria, the ship that sailed the ocean (the "crystalline zodiac") as the carriage of the sun sails the zodiac, and finally encountered the Strait of Magellan. The "pillars" refer to the Pillars of Hercules (Strait of Gibraltar), the "scarlet hanging" the color of the sky at dawn: that is, west and east.

De firmes islas no la inmóvil flota
en aquel mar del Alba te describo,
cuyo número—ya que no lascivo—
por lo bello, agradable y por lo vario
la dulce confusión hacer podía,
que en los blancos estanques del Eurota
la virginal desnuda montería,
haciendo escollos o de mármol pario
o de terso marfil sus miembros bellos,
490   que pudo bien Acteón perderse en ellos.

El bosque dividido en islas pocas,
fragante productor de aquel aroma
—que, traducido mal por el Egito,
tarde le encomendó el Nilo a sus bocas,
y ellas más tarde a la gulosa Grecia—,
clavo no, espuela sí del apetito
—que cuanto en conocelle tardó Roma
fué templado Catón, casta Lucrecia—,
quédese, amigo, en tan inciertos mares,
500   donde con mi hacienda
del alma se quedó la mejor prenda,
cuya memoria es bueitre de pesares.»

    En suspiros con esto,
y en más anegó lágrimas el resto
de su discurso el montañés prolijo,
que el viento su caudal, el mar su hijo.

Consolallo pudiera el peregrino
con las de su edad corta historias largas,

I will not describe the unmoving fleet
of fixed isles in that Orient sea of Dawn,[1]
whose number—though not lasciviousness—
in beauty, delight, and in variety
   might cause the sweet confusion
that in the white pools of the Eurotas
was caused by virginal nude huntresses,
their beautiful limbs creating reefs of
Parian marble or of smoothest ivory,
that well might Actaeon be lost in them.[2]   490

The forest divided among the several isles,
   fragrant source of the scent[3]
—which, in arduous transport throughout Egypt,
the Nile commended late to all its mouths,
and even later they to gluttonous Greece—,
not nail of clove but spur to appetite
—for as long as Rome did not know of it
Cato was temperate and Lucretia chaste—
let it remain, my friend, in uncertain seas,
   where along with my fortune   500
the most precious gem of my soul remained,
his memory a vulture of woe and grief."[4]

   And here the prolix highlander
   drowned in more sighs and more tears
   the remainder of his tale
than winds that took his wealth or seas his son.

   The wanderer might have offered him comfort
with lengthy stories of his own brief life

---

1 The allusion is to the islands of Oceania (Australasia). 2 The Eurotas is a river in Sparta. The hunter Actaeon came upon Diana and her nymphs bathing there. As punishment he was turned into a stag, then torn apart by his own dogs. 3 The Moluccas, or Spice Islands, that produce cloves (the word in Spanish refers to nails as well as the spice). 4 The mountain man lost his son, his "most precious gem," at sea.

si—vinculados todos a sus cargas,
cual próvidas hormigas a sus mieses—
no comenzaran ya los montañeses
a esconder con el número el camino,
y el cielo con el polvo. Enjugó el viejo
del tierno humor las venerables canas,
y levantando al forastero, dijo:

«Cabo me han hecho, hijo,
deste hermoso tercio de serranas;
si tu neutralidad sufre consejo,
y no te fuerza obligación precisa,
la piedad que en mi alma ya te hospeda
hoy te convida al que nos guarda sueño
      política alameda,
verde muro de aquel lugar pequeño
que, a pesar de esos fresnos, se divisa;
sigue la femenil tropa conmigo:
verás curioso y honrarás testigo
el tálamo de nuestros labradores,
que de tu calidad señas mayores
me dan que del Océano tus paños,
o razón falta donde sobran años.»

Mal pudo el extranjero, agradecido,
en tercio tal negar tal compañía
y en tan noble ocasión tal hospedaje.
Alegres pisan la que, si no era
de chopos calle y de álamos carrera,
el fresco de los céfiros rüido,
el denso de los árboles celaje,
en duda ponen cuál mayor hacía
guerra al calor o resistencia al día.

Coros tejiendo, voces alternando,
sigue la dulce escuadra montañesa
del perezoso arroyo el paso lento,
      en cuanto él hurta blando,

if—all bound to their burdens
like provident ants to their grains of wheat—   *510*
the mountain men had not already begun
to obscure and hide the path with their numbers
and heaven with their dust. The old man wiped
from venerable white hair his aching tears
and, helping the stranger to stand, he said:

"They have made me head, my son,
of this legion of beauteous mountain girls;
if indetermination endures advice,
and clear obligation does not press on you,
the pity that lodges you in my soul   *520*
today invites you to the sleep awaiting
    in a benign promenade,
    green wall of the hamlet small
that, despite those poplar trees, is visible;
follow the feminine troop along with me:
you will see the curious nuptial chamber
of our peasants, honor it with your presence,
for your clothes offer greater traces of rank
    than of the ocean boundless,
or my misjudgment is greater than my years."   *530*

The stranger, filled with gratitude, scarce could
refuse such a companion in this troop,
such lodging for so virtuous an event.
    Joyful they walk though there is
no street of black poplars, of aspens no road;
    the cool whisper of zephyrs,
    the dense interweave of trees
cast doubt on which waged greater war, resisted
    more the heat and light of day.

Weaving choruses, alternating voices,   *540*
the sweet mountain troop
follows the slow pace of the lazy stream,
    while it, so gentle, steals

43

entre los olmos que robustos besa,
pedazos de cristal, que el movimiento
libra en la falda, en el coturno ella,
 de la coluna bella,
 ya que celosa basa,
dispensadora del cristal no escasa.

550

Sirenas de los montes su concento,
a la que menos del sañudo viento
 pudiera antigua planta
temer rüina o recelar fracaso,
pasos hiciera dar el menor paso
 de su pie o su garganta.

Pintadas aves—cítaras de pluma—
coronaban la bárbara capilla,
mientras el arroyuelo para oílla
 hace de blanca espuma

560

tantas orejas cuantas guijas lava,
de donde es fuente adonde arroyo acaba.

Vencedores se arrogan los serranos
los consignados premios otro día,
ya al formidable salto, ya a la ardiente
lucha, ya a la carrera polvorosa.
El menos ágil, cuantos comarcanos
convoca el caso, él solo desafía,
consagrando los palios a su esposa,
 que a mucha fresca rosa

570

beber el sudor hace de su frente,
 mayor aún del que espera
en la lucha, en el salto, en la carrera.

Centro apacible un círculo espacioso
a más caminos que una estrella rayos,
hacía, bien de pobos, bien de alisos,

from among the robust elms it kisses
lengths of crystal that motion
frees between skirt and cothurn,[1]
    jealous base of the beautiful column,
though not a scant presenter of the crystal.

Sirens of the mountains their sweet harmonies,
the ancient trees that have least cause to dread   *550*
    ruin or fear a downfall
    from the wind raging cruel,
would step to follow the least change of pace
    in their feet, or from those throats.

    Bright-hued birds—feathered zithers—
crowned the wild rustic chapel,
while to hear, the rushing brook
makes ears of foaming white spume
round each smooth stone it washes
from its source to where it courses as a stream.   *560*

The mountain men already claim their triumph,
the wreaths of laurel prepared for the next day,
whether in arduous leap, or passionate
    combat, or footrace's dust.
The least agile of the neighboring lads
invited to the wedding defies them all,
consecrating the prizes to his wife,
    who with many a fresh rose
soaks up the perspiration from his brow,
    greater than what he expects   *570*
in the combat, in the leap, and in the race.

A spacious circle made a peaceful center
for more avenues than a star has beams
of white poplars or perhaps of alders,

---

1 "Lengths of crystal" refer to the girls' legs, revealed as they dance; a "cothurn" is a boot.

donde la Primavera,
—calzada abriles y vestida mayos—
centellas saca de cristal undoso
a un pedernal orlado de narcisos.
580   Este, pues, centro era
meta umbrosa al vaquero convecino,
y delicioso término al distante,
donde, aún cansado más que el caminante,
      concurría el camino.

Al concento se abaten cristalino
      sedientas las serranas,
cual simples codornices al reclamo
que les miente la voz, y verde cela,
entre la no espigada mies, la tela.
590   Músicas hojas viste el menor ramo
del álamo que peina verdes canas;
no céfiros en él, no ruiseñores
lisonjear pudieron breve rato
      al montañés, que—ingrato
al fresco, a la armonía y a las flores—
      del sitio pisa ameno
la fresca hierba, cual la arena ardiente
de la Libia, y a cuantas da la fuente
sierpes de aljófar, aún mayor veneno
600   que a las del Ponto, tímido, atribuye,
según el pie, según los labios huye.

Pasaron todos pues, y regulados
cual en los equinocios surcar vemos
los piélagos del aire libre algunas
      volantes no galeras,
      sino grullas veleras,
tal vez creciendo, tal menguando lunas

and this is where the Spring
   —shod in Aprils, clad in Mays—
brings the gleam of crystal waves[1]
to flinty rock rimmed round with jonquil blooms.
   This center, then, the shaded
destination was of cowherds proximal,   580
delicious object of those come from afar,
where, even more weary than the traveler,
      the road came to a rest.

To sweet crystal harmony
   thirsting mountain girls kneel down,
   like foolish quail to the call
that appears to be their voice, and green conceals
the net that lies among the spiky grains.
Musical leaves adorn the smallest branch
of the poplar combing out its green white hair;   590
   no zephyrs, no nightingales
could cajole even for the briefest while
   the mountain man—unthankful
for the coolness, the harmony, the flowers—
   who treads in that pleasant place
cool grass as if it were the burning sand
of Libya, and the serpents of pearl fallen
from the fountain as if more venomous
than those of Pontus, and fearful, it seems,
keeping his feet, his lips, at a remove.[2]   600

And so they all passed by, and in good order
as at the equinox we see furrowing
      through oceans of open air
      not flights of galley ships
      but flocks of swift-sailing cranes,
moons perhaps waxing, perhaps on the wane

1 That is, a spring.   2 The men avoid the fountain as if the serpentine rivu-
lets of water were the poisonous snakes of the Black Sea (Pontus).

sus distantes extremos,
caracteres tal vez formando alados
610 en el papel diáfano del cielo
las plumas de su vuelo.

Ellas en tanto en bóvedas de sombras,
pintadas siempre al fresco,
cubren las que sidón telar turquesco
no ha sabido imitar verdes alfombras.

Apenas reclinaron la cabeza,
cuando, en número iguales y en belleza,
los márgenes matiza de las fuentes
segunda primavera de villanas,
620 que—parientas del novio aun más cercanas
que vecinos sus pueblos—de presentes
prevenidas, concurren a las bodas.

Mezcladas hacen todas
teatro dulce—no de escena muda—
el apacible sitio: espacio breve
en que, a pesar del sol, cuajada nieve,
y nieve de colores mil vestida,
la sombra vió florida
en la hierba menuda.

630 Viendo, pues, que igualmente les quedaba
para el lugar a ellas de camino
lo que al Sol para el lóbrego occidente,
cual de aves se caló turba canora
a robusto nogal que acequia lava
en cercado vecino,
cuando a nuestros antípodas la Aurora
las rosas gozar deja de su frente:

their most distant extremes,
perhaps forming letters on the pellucid
    paper of the heavens with
    the quill feathers of their flight.   610

Meanwhile mountain girls under vaults of shade,
    ever painted al fresco,
hide green carpet even Turkish weavers in
    Sidon[1] cannot duplicate.

No sooner had they reclined their heads than
    in equal numbers and beauty
a second springtime of mountain maidens
brings color to the edges of the fountain,
who—kin to the bridegroom even closer
than to their nearby hamlets—well supplied with   620
    gifts, gather for the wedding.

    All of them together form
a sweet theater—no mute pantomimed scene—
    in that pleasant place: brief time
when, in spite of the sun, the firm-shaped snow,[2]
snow dressed in a thousand hues, the flowering
    shade saw on the common grass.

Seeing, then, that they needed the same time
    to walk to the village as
the Sun to come to the gloom of Occident,   630
like a sweet-voiced flock of birds that settles
on a robust walnut tree bathed by channeled
    water in a nearby field
when Aurora allows our antipodes
to delight in the roses on her brow:[3]

---

1 A Phoenician city located on the Lebanese coast.   2 The white-as-snow
limbs of the colorfully dressed girls on the grass.   3 Twilight means that it
is dawn on the other side of the world (the antipodes).

tal sale aquella que sin alas vuela
hermosa escuadra con ligero paso,
640   haciéndole atalayas del ocaso
cuantos humeros cuenta la aldehuela.

El lento escuadrón luego
alcanzan de serranos,
y—disolviendo allí la compañía—
al pueblo llegan con la luz que el día
cedió al sacro volcán de errante fuego,
a la torre, de luces coronada,
que el templo ilustra, y a los aires vanos
artificiosamente da exhalada
650   luminosas de pólvora saetas,
purpúreos no cometas.

Los fuegos, pues, el joven solemniza,
mientras el viejo tanta acusa tea
al de las bodas dios, no alguna sea
de nocturno Faetón carroza ardiente,
y miserablemente
campo amanezca estéril de ceniza
la que anocheció aldea.

De Alcides le llevó luego a las plantas,
660   que estaban, no muy lejos,
trenzándose el cabello verde a cuantas
da el fuego luces y el arroyo espejos.
Tanto garzón robusto,
tanta ofrecen los álamos zagala,

that is how the beautiful unwinged band
　　flies away with agile step,
making watchtowers for the setting sun
of smoking chimneys in the tiny hamlet.

　　Soon they overtake the　　　　　　　　　　　640
　　slow-moving troop of men,
　　and—parting company there[1]—
they come to the village with the light that day
ceded to the sacred volcano of
errant fire on the tower crowned in lights
that illumines the temple,[2] and in vain air
　　sends off the exhaled powder
of arrows luminous through artifice,
　　rather than purple comets.

The young man, then, celebrates the fires,　　　650
while the old faults the god of weddings for
　　too many torches, the risk
that one becomes the burning coach of Phaethon[3]
and into a woefully barren field
of ash mutates what once had been a village.

He led him to the trees of Alcides,[4]
　　not very far away,
arranging their green tresses in the lights
of the fires, in the mirrors of the stream.
　　So many robust lads　　　　　　　　　　　660
among the poplars, so many country maids,

1 The word "there" is ambiguous; it isn't clear whether it refers to the coun-
tryside or to the village.　2 The villagers are setting off rockets from the
church tower to celebrate the wedding.　3 The son of Helios, Phaethon per-
suaded his father to let him drive the Sun's chariot across the sky. He couldn't
control the horses and came so close to the earth he almost destroyed
it.　4 Poplars were sacred to Alcides. Phaethon's sisters were turned into
poplars as part of Jupiter's punishment of their brother.

que abrevïara el Sol en una estrella,
    por ver la menos bella,
cuantos saluda rayos el bengala,
    del Ganges cisne adusto.

La gaita al baile solicita el gusto,
    a la voz el salterio;
cruza el Trión más fijo el hemisferio,
y el tronco mayor danza en la ribera;
    el eco, voz ya entera,
no hay silencio a que pronto no responda;
fanal es del arroyo cada onda,
luz el reflejo, la agua vidrïera.

Términos le da el sueño al regocijo,
mas al cansancio no: que el movimiento
verdugo de las fuerzas es prolijo.
Los fuegos—cuyas lenguas, ciento a ciento,
desmintieron la noche algunas horas,
cuyas luces, del sol competidoras,
fingieron día en la tiniebla oscura—
murieron, y en sí mismos sepultados,
sus miembros, en cenizas desatados,
piedras son de su misma sepultura.

Vence la noche al fin, y triunfa mudo
el silencio, aunque breve, del rüido:
sólo gime ofendido
    el sagrado laurel del hierro agudo;
deja de su esplendor, deja desnudo

670

680

690

that to see the least comely
the Sun gladly would shrink into a star
    all the beams the Bengal greets,
    sable swan of the Ganges.[1]

The bagpipe invites one's joy to the dance,
    the psaltery to song;
the most fixed Trion[2] crosses the hemisphere,
and the thickest trunk dances on the bank;
    echo, now with entire voice[3]   670
    responds to every silence;
each ripple in the stream becomes a lantern,
the reflection light, of glass the water.

Sleep puts an end to the joy and revelry
but not to weariness: the long exertion
is executioner to all their strength.
    The fires—whose tongues denied
    night utterly for hours,
whose lights, in competition with the sun
    feigned day in shadowy dark—   680
    died, and buried in themselves
    their limbs, crumbled into ash,
    on their own graves are the stones.

Night conquers in the end, and mute silence,
    though brief, triumphs over sound:
    only the sacred laurel, offended,
    touched by sharp metal, moans;[4]
stripping away its splendor, stripping away

---

1 Because it is night, the Sun cannot watch the scene, but to do so would gladly reduce all his rays to a single star, depriving the other side of the world of dawn. 2 A "fixed star" in the constellation Ursa Major. 3 The celebration was so great that echo repeated entire words, not merely their endings. 4 The trees are cut down to decorate the village and create the appearance of forests and alamedas.

de su frondosa pompa al verde aliso
   el golpe no remiso
   del villano membrudo;
   el que resistir pudo
al animoso Austro, al Euro ronco,
chopo gallardo—cuyo liso tronco
papel fué de pastores, aunque rudo—
a revelar secretos va a la aldea,
que impide Amor que aun otro chopo lea.

Estos árboles, pues, ve la mañana
mentir florestas, y emular viales
cuantos muró de líquidos cristales
   agricultura urbana.

Recordó al Sol, no, de su espuma cana,
la dulce de las aves armonía,
sino los dos topacios que batía
—orientales aldabas—Himeneo.
   Del carro, pues, febeo
   el luminoso tiro,
mordiendo oro, el eclíptico zafiro
pisar quería, cuando el populoso
   lugarillo, el serrano
con su huésped, que admira cortesano
—a pesar del estambre y de la seda—
   el que tapiz frondoso
tejió de verdes hojas la arboleda,
y los que por las calles espaciosas
   fabrican arcos, rosas:
oblicuos nuevos, pénsiles jardines,
de tantos como víolas jazmines.

all the leafy pomp from the alder green
   with the merciless blows   690
   of powerful country lads;
   gallant, able to withstand
Auster the spirited, raucous Eurus,[1]
   the black poplar—its smooth trunk
paper was for the shepherds, although crude—
goes to the village to reveal secrets Love
did not allow e'en other poplars to read.[2]

   The morning, then, sees these trees
feigning forests, emulating avenues
   enwalled in liquid crystal   700
   by farming most urbane.

From his foaming couch the Sun was wakened
not by the dulcet harmonies of birds,
but by two topazes struck together
—clappers on the door of Orient—by Hymen.
   Then, of the Phoebean
   carriage[3] the luminous team,
   biting on gold, wished to step
   on the sapphire ecliptic[4]
when in the populous hamlet the mountain   710
   man and his courtly guest who
marvels—no matter worsted and silk—at
the abundant tapestry of its green leaves
   woven by the shaded grove,
and arches of roses along the broad streets:
   new slanting, hanging gardens,
   of violets and jasmines.[5]

---

1 The southeast wind. 2 Shepherds would carve amorous secrets on the bark of the black poplars. 3 The chariot of the Sun (also called Phoebus). 4 The ecliptic is the path across the sky that the Sun seems to follow in the course of a year. 5 The hamlet is "populous" because of the wedding guests, and it is decorated with trees and flowers (like the hanging gardens of Babylon) for the celebration.

Al galán novio el montañés presenta
su forastero; luego al venerable
padre de la que en sí bella se esconde
con ceño dulce, y, con silencio afable,
beldad parlera, gracia muda ostenta:
cual del rizado verde botón donde
abrevia su hermosura virgen rosa,
    las cisuras cairela
730   un color que la púrpura que cela
por brújula concede vergonzosa.
    Digna la juzga esposa
de un héroe, si no augusto, esclarecido,
el joven, al instante arrebatado
a la que, naufragante y desterrado,
    lo condenó a su olvido.

Este, pues, Sol que a olvido lo condena,
cenizas hizo las que su memoria
negras plumas vistió, que infelizmente
740   sordo engendran gusano, cuyo diente,
minador antes lento de su gloria,
inmortal arador fué de su pena.
Y en la sombra no más de la azucena,
que del clavel procura acompañada
imitar en la bella labradora
el templado color de la que adora,
víbora pisa tal el pensamiento,
que el alma, por los ojos desatada,
señas diera de su arrebatamiento,
750   si de zampoñas ciento
y de otros, aunque bárbaros, sonoros
instrumentos, no, en dos festivos coros,
vírgenes bellas, jóvenes lucidos,
    llegaran conducidos.

The old man presents to the gallant groom
his stranger; then to the venerable
father of the girl, who conceals herself 720
in herself with a sweet frown, and, affably
silent, voluble beauty displays mute grace:
    just as in the curled green bud
where the virgin rose constricts its loveliness,
    the commissures are edged
in a color it conceals, the purple
conceded by a shameless aperture.
    Deeming her the espoused
of a hero, if not royal then renowned,
    the young man's thoughts forthwith turn 730
    to the one[1] who condemned him
to be forgotten, banished, and shipwrecked.

This Sun who condemns him to be forgotten,
made ashes of ebon plumes his memory
    wore, and they unhappily
engender a noiseless worm, whose tooth,
once an unhurried sapper of his glory,
becomes an immortal plowshare of his grief.
And in the mere shadow of the lily white
    that with the carnation strives 740
in the lovely peasant to emulate
the modulated hue of one he adores,
    his thought treads on a viper
and so his soul, unleashed through his eyes,
would have revealed signs of his deepest passion
    if two festive choruses,
    lovely virgins, comely youths,
accompanied by panpipes in their hundreds
and other, although primitive, still sonorous
    instruments, had not arrived. 750

---

1 The "one," the "Sun," is the woman who scorned the stranger (and the
reason for his shipwreck) and causes him to burn in his grief ("ebon plumes")
like the phoenix.

El numeroso al fin de labradores
   concurso impacïente
los novios saca: él, de años floreciente,
y de caudal más floreciente que ellos;
ella, la misma pompa de las flores,
760   la esfera misma de los rayos bellos.
   El lazo de ambos cuellos
entre un lascivo enjambre iba de amores
   Himeneo añudando,
mientras invocan su deidad la alterna
de zagalejas cándidas voz tierna
y de garzones este acento blando:

CORO I

Ven, Himeneo, ven donde te espera
con ojos y sin alas un Cupido,
cuyo cabello intonso dulcemente
770   niega el vello que el vulto ha colorido:
el vello, flores de su primavera,
y rayos el cabello de su frente.
Niño amó la que adora adolescente,
villana Psiques, ninfa labradora
de la tostada Ceres. Esta, ahora,
en los inciertos de su edad segunda
crepúsculos, vincule tu coyunda
   a su ardiente deseo.
Ven, Himeneo, ven; ven, Himeneo.

At last the numerous gathering of
   peasants grown impatient
brings out bride and groom: he, flourishing in years,
and in his wealth more flourishing than they;
she, the very splendor of the flowers,
   the orb of beautiful beams.
   The loop around both necks,
amid a playful swarm of other loves,
   Hymen ties in a knot,
while the marriage god is summoned back and forth   *760*
by tender voices of the guileless maids,
   gentle accents of the lads:

CHORUS I

Come, Hymen, come to where a Cupid sighted
   and unwinged[1] awaits you,
   his unshorn locks so sweetly
deny the down tinting his lineaments:
   the down, blossoms of his spring,
   and beams the curls on his brow.
As a boy, he loved the one he adores
as a youth, village Psyche,[2] peasant nymph   *770*
   of nut-brown Ceres. Let her,
now, in the uncertain twilights of second
   age,[3] link your marriage tie
   to his burning desire.
   Come, Hymen, come; Hymen come.

---

1 Cupid, or Love, is traditionally depicted as blindfolded and having wings. 2 The groom is called Cupid, who fell in love with the nymph Psyche. The bride is called a nymph of Ceres, goddess of the earth's fertility, because the girl is a peasant. 3 The bride is in early adolescence.

CORO II

780 Ven, Himeneo, donde, entre arreboles
de honesto rosicler, previene el día
—aurora de sus ojos soberanos—
virgen tan bella, que hacer podría
tórrida la Noruega con dos soles,
y blanca la Etiopia con dos manos.
Claveles del abril, rubíes tempranos,
cuantos engasta el oro del cabello,
cuantas—del uno ya y del otro cuello
cadenas—la concordia engaza rosas,
790 de sus mejillas, siempre vergonzosas,
    purpúreo son trofeo.
Ven, Himeneo, ven; ven, Himeneo.

CORO I

Ven, Himeneo, y plumas no vulgares
al aire los hijuelos den alados
de las que el bosque bellas ninfas cela;
de sus carcajes, éstos, argentados,
flechen mosquetas, nieven azahares;
vigilantes aquéllos, la aldehuela
rediman del que más o tardo vuela,
800 o infausto gime pájaro nocturno;
mudos coronen otros por su turno
el dulce lecho conjugal, en cuanto
lasciva abeja al virginal acanto
    néctar le chupa hibleo.
Ven, Himeneo, ven; ven, Himeneo.

CHORUS II

Come, Hymen, come where, among rose-red clouds,
    a chaste russet day foretells
    —aurora to her sovereign eyes—
a virgin so beautiful she could make
    Norway torrid with two suns,[1]   780
Ethiopia white with her two hands.
Carnations of April, early rubies,
    set in the gold of her hair,
chains—looped round one neck and round the other—
    harmony links with roses,
    of her always modest cheeks
    they are the purple trophy.
    Come, Hymen, come; Hymen come.

CHORUS I

Come, Hymen, come, and let the least common
amoretti of nymphs the forest hides   790
    take wing, feathers in the air,
    and from their silver quivers
let some bring down a shower of wild roses,
    a snow of orange blossoms;
    and others guard the village,
protect it from the accursed birds of night
    that soon or late fly, or shriek;
    let others, mute, in turn crown
    the sweet conjugal bed, as
    the groom, lascivious bee,   800
    sips Hiblean nectar[2]
    from acanthus virginal.
    Come, Hymen, come; Hymen come.

---

1 That is, her eyes.   2 The Hiblean Mountains, in Sicily. The image evokes the couple's first kiss.

CORO II

Ven, Himeneo, y las volantes pías
que azules ojos con pestañas de oro
sus plumas son, conduzgan alta diosa,
gloria mayor del soberano coro.
810   Fíe tus nudos ella, que los días
disuelvan tarde en senectud dichosa;
y la que Juno es hoy a nuestra esposa,
casta Lucina—en lunas desiguales—
tantas veces repita sus umbrales,
que Níobe inmortal la admire el mundo,
no en blanco mármol, por su mal fecundo,
    escollo hoy del Leteo.
Ven, Himeneo, ven; ven, Himeneo.

CORO I

Ven, Himeneo, y nuestra agricultura
820   de copia tal a estrellas deba amigas
progenie tan robusta, que su mano
toros dome, y de un rubio mar de espigas
inunde liberal la tierra dura;
y al verde, joven, floreciente llano
blancas ovejas suyas hagan, cano,
en breves horas caducar la hierba;
oro le expriman líquido a Minerva,
y—los olmos casando con las vides—
mientras coronan pámpanos a Alcides

CHORUS II

Come, Hymen, come, and the flying piebalds
whose feathers are blue eyes, lashes of gold,
let them transport the lofty goddess, greatest
     glory of the sovereign choir.[1]
May she be surety to the knots you tie,
and may the days dissolve them in blissful age;
and may she who Juno is today to our   810
bride, as chaste Lucina[2]—in unequal moons—
     so often cross her threshold
that the world admires a Niobe[3]
immortal, not, to her sorrow, fecund,
white marble now, outcropping in the Lethe.
     Come, Hymen, come; Hymen come.

CHORUS I

Come, Hymen, come, let our agriculture so
     prosper under auspicious
stars, with progeny so robust their hands
tame brave bulls, and in a blond sea of wheat   820
     liberally flood hard earth;
and may herds of their sheep turn the flowering
     green hair of the plain white,
     in brief hours aging the grass;
let them of Minerva press the liquid gold,[4]
and—wedding elms to grapevines—
as Alcides is crowned with leaves and tendrils

---

1 Peacocks pull the carriage of Juno, queen of Olympus.   2 Lucina, one of
the aspects of Juno, was the protector of childbirth.   3 Niobe boasted of
the number of children she had and was punished by the gods by being
turned into a weeping stone. Góngora alters the story slightly, making her a
slab of marble in the Lethe, the river of oblivion in Hades.   4 The olive (and
its oil) was sacred to Minerva, the goddess of wisdom.

830   clava empuñe Liëo.
Ven, Himeneo, ven; ven, Himeneo.

CORO II

Ven, Himeneo, y tantas le dé a Pales
cuantas a Palas dulces prendas esta
apenas hija hoy, madre mañana.
De errantes lilios unas la floresta
cubran: corderos mil, que los cristales
vistan del río en breve undosa lana;
de Aracnes otras la arrogancia vana
modestas acusando en blancas telas,
840   no los hurtos de amor, no las cautelas
de Júpiter compulsen: que, aun en lino,
ni a la pluvia luciente de oro fino,
     ni al blanco cisne creo.
Ven, Himeneo, ven; ven, Himeneo.

   El dulce alterno canto
a sus umbrales revocó felices
los novios, del vecino templo santo.
Del yugo aún no domadas las cervices,
novillos—breve término surcado—
850   restituyen así el pendiente arado
al que pajizo albergue los aguarda.

Llegaron todos pues, y, con gallarda
civil magnificencia, el suegro anciano,

Lyaeus wields the cudgel.[1]
Come, Hymen, come; Hymen, come.

CHORUS II

Come, Hymen, come, and may she offer Pales   830
as many sweet darlings as she does to Pallas,[2]
barely daughter today, tomorrow mother.
Let some cover the woods with errant lilies:
thousands of lambs, dressing the river crystal
   in short, tightly curling wool;
let others, modest, depict the arrogance
   of Arachne[3] on white cloth,
but not love's abductions, the wiles of Jupiter:
let them not trust, even on spun linen
either the shining shower of fine gold   840
   or the swan's snow-white feathers:[4]
   Come, Hymen, come; Hymen, come.

The sweet alternating song
called to their threshold from the nearby holy
   temple the joyful couple.
   Necks not yet tamed by the yoke,
   calves—a small plot furrowed—
   that return the still-hitched plow
to the straw-covered shelter that awaits them.

Then all the guests arrived, and with gallant   850
courtesy, magnanimous, the ancient
   father-in-law to the groom

1 Elms were sacred to Alcides, as grapevines were to Bacchus (Lyaeus). In
this image, the two exchange attributes.   2 Pales was the patron of shep-
herds, Pallas (Minerva) of weavers.   3 Arachne, a weaver, depicted the
amours of the gods, antagonized Pallas, and was turned into a spider.
4 Jupiter turned himself into a swan to make love to Leda and into a shower
of gold to possess Danae.

cuantos la sierra dió, cuantos dió el llano
  labradores convida
a la prolija rústica comida
que sin rumor previno en mesas grandes.

Ostente crespas blancas esculturas
artífice gentil de dobladuras
860 en los que damascó manteles Flandes,
mientras casero lino Ceres tanta
ofrece ahora, cuantos guardó el heno
dulces pomos, que al curso de Atalanta
  fueran dorado freno.

Manjares que el veneno
y el apetito ignoran igualmente,
les sirvieron, y en oro, no, luciente,
confuso Baco, ni en bruñida plata
  su néctar les desata,
870 sino en vidrio topacios carmesíes
  y pálidos rubíes.

Sellar del fuego quiso regalado
los gulosos estómagos el rubio,
imitador süave de la cera,
quesillo—dulcemente apremïado
  de rústica, vaquera,
blanca, hermosa mano, cuyas venas
la distinguieron de la leche apenas—;
mas ni la encarcelada nuez esquiva,
880 ni el membrillo pudieran anudado,
  si la sabrosa oliva
no serenara el bacanal diluvio.

invites all from the mountain, all from the plain
    to the bounteous rustic meal
that soundless was brought to the long tables.

Let the courtly artifice of folds and pleats
    boast of complex sculptures white
    on damask cloths of Flanders;
here Ceres offers now on homespun linen
all the sweet pomes lying in the grass that   *860*
    served as golden bit, as reins
    in Atalanta's race.[1]

Dishes unknown to venom
    or to voracity were served,
Bacchus did not his pleasing nectar obscure
in gleaming gold or burnished silver but
    let it pour into glass
turned crimson topazes and rubies pale.

Delicate and blond, a soft aper of wax,
    a cheese—sweetly shaped by   *870*
    a rustic, cow-tending,
    beautiful white hand, whose veins
    scarce distinguished it from milk—
wished to quench the fire in gluttonous stomachs,
but neither the aloof, the cloistered nutmeat,
    nor the quince could succeed;
    only the savory olive could still
    the Bacchanalian flood.[2]

---

1 Atalanta challenged all suitors to a race. If the man won, she would marry him; if he lost, he would die. Either Melanion or Hippomenes, depending on the version, obtained golden apples from Venus, threw them in Atalanta's path, distracted her, and won.   2 Dámaso Alonso, the editor of the Spanish edition used for this translation, points out that the olive branch signaled the end of the flood for Noah, just as the olive stills the effects of the wine.

Levantadas las mesas, al canoro
son de la ninfa un tiempo, ahora caña,
seis de los montes, seis de la campaña,
—sus espaldas rayando el sutil oro
que negó al viento el nácar bien tejido—
terno de gracias bello, repetido
cuatro veces en doce labradoras,
890   entró bailando numerosamente;
y dulce musa entre ellas—si consiente
bárbaras el Parnaso moradoras—
    «Vivid felices», dijo,
«largo curso de edad nunca prolijo;
y si prolijo, en nudos amorosos
    siempre vivid, esposos.
Venza no solo en su candor la nieve,
mas plata en su esplendor sea cardada
cuanto estambre vital Cloto os traslada
900   de la alta fatal rueca al huso breve.

    Sean de la Fortuna
    aplausos la respuesta
    de vuestras granjerías.
    A la reja importuna,
    a la azada molesta
fecundo os rinda—en desiguales días—
    el campo agradecido
oro trillado y néctar exprimido.

    Sus morados cantuesos, sus copadas
910   encinas la montaña contar antes
deje que vuestras cabras, siempre errantes,
que vuestras vacas, tarde o nunca herradas.

The tables cleared, to the melodious
　　sound of nymph once, now reed,[1]　　　　　　*880*
six from the mountains and six from the plains,
　　—their backs veined with subtle gold
that well-woven nacre denied to the wind[2]—
a lovely triad of graces, repeated
　　four times by twelve peasant girls,
　　entered dancing in rhythm;
and a sweet muse among them—if Parnassus[3]
gives its consent to denizens more rough-hewn—
　　spoke and said, "Live happily
a long and never wearisome span of time;　　　*890*
and if wearisome, live always in loving
　　bonds, yoked as husband and wife.
May any vital thread that Clotho[4] spins
for you, from her high fatal distaff to the
brief spindle, surpass in candor the snow,
　　in carded splendor silver.

　　May the response of Fortune
　　to your farming be applause.
　　To the importune plow,
　　to the troublesome hoe　　　　　　　　　*900*
　　may a grateful field produce
　　for you—in uneven days—
　　well-threshed gold and nectar pressed.[5]

May the purple lavender, the thick-crowned
oaks in the mountain be counted before your
　　goats, forever errant, your
　　cows, branded never or late.

1 Syrinx, a nymph pursued by Pan, asked to be turned into a reed, which
Pan then used to make his flute.　2 That is, their long blond hair is tied up
with ribbons the color of mother-of-pearl.　3 The home of Apollo and the
Muses.　4 One of the three Fates who spin the threads of human des-
tiny.　5 That is, wheat and olive oil.

Corderillos os brote la ribera,
      que la hierba menuda
y las perlas exceda del rocío
      su número, y del río
la blanca espuma, cuantos la tijera
      vellones les desnuda.

Tantos de breve fábrica, aunque ruda,
albergues vuestros las abejas moren,
y primaveras tantas os desfloren,
que—cual la Arabia madre ve de aromas
sacros troncos sudar fragantes gomas—
      vuestros corchos por uno y otro poro
en dulce se desaten líquido oro.

Próspera, al fin, mas no espumosa tanto,
      vuestra fortuna sea,
que alimenten la invidia en nuestra aldea
áspides más que en la región del llanto.
Entre opulencias y necesidades,
medianías vinculen competentes
      a vuestros descendientes
—previniendo ambos daños—las edades.
Ilustren obeliscos las ciudades,
a los rayos de Júpiter expuesta
—aún más que a los de Febo—su corona,
cuando a la choza pastoral perdona
el cielo, fulminando la floresta.

Cisnes pues una y otra pluma, en esta
tranquilidad os halle labradora
      la postrimera hora:
cuya lámina cifre desengaños,
que en letras pocas lean muchos años.»

Del himno culto dió el último acento
fin mudo al baile, al tiempo que seguida
la novia sale de villanas ciento
a la verde florida palizada,

At the riverbanks may you have so many
    lambs that their number exceeds
    common grass and pearls of dew,   910
    may the fleece the scissors shears
    transcend the river's white foam.

May bees dwell in so many of your hives
    of small construction, though rough,
and deflower so many springs for you, that,
—as Arabia, mother of aromas,
watches her sacred trunks drip fragrant gums—
may your cork trees pour forth from every pore
    that sweet, that liquid gold.

    May your fortunes prosper, but   920
be not so lush that in our village more asps
feed on envy than in the pit of woe.
    Between want and opulence
may the years to your descendants proffer
—avoiding both those evils—a middle ground.
Let obelisks adorn the distant cities,
their crowns exposed to the bolts of Jupiter
    —more than to Phoebus's rays—
while heaven pardons the pastoral hut
    and strikes the forest instead.   930

    Both of you with swans' plumage,[1]
and in this rustic tranquility may
    your final hour find you:
let your epitaph epitomize the truth
that in scant letters future years can read."

The final accent of the learned hymn
brought the dancing to a silent close as
the bride, at the head of countless peasant girls,
goes to the enclosure green and flowering,

1 That is, with the white hair of age.

cual nueva fénix en flamantes plumas
matutinos del sol rayos vestida,
de cuanta surca el aire acompañada
 monarquía canora;
y, vadeando nubes, las espumas
del rey corona de los otros ríos:
en cuya orilla el viento hereda ahora
 pequeños no vacíos
de funerales bárbaros trofeos
que el Egipto erigió a sus Ptolomeos.

Los árboles que el bosque habían fingido,
umbroso coliseo ya formando,
 despejan el ejido,
 olímpica palestra
de valientes desnudos labradores.

Llegó la desposada apenas, cuando
 feroz ardiente muestra
hicieron dos robustos luchadores
de sus músculos, menos defendidos
del blanco lino que del vello obscuro.
Abrazáronse, pues, los dos, y luego
—humo anhelando el que no suda fuego—
de recíprocos nudos impedidos
cual duros olmos de implicantes vides,
yedra el uno es tenaz del otro muro.
Mañosos, al fin, hijos de la tierra,
 cuando fuertes no Alcides,
procuran derribarse, y, derribados,
cual pinos se levantan arraigados
en los profundos senos de la sierra.
Premio los honra igual. Y de otros cuatro

like a new phoenix dressed in plumes as brilliant   940
as rays of the morning sun, accompanied
    by the lyric monarchy
that cuts through air and, fording clouds, crowns with foam
    the king of all the rivers:[1]
on its banks now the wind inherits trophies
    deserted and not small
    of barbarous funeral rites
erected by Egypt for her Ptolemies.

    The trees that had feigned a wood,
    cleared away from the pasture   950
and forming now a shaded coliseum,
    Olympian palestra
for peasant lads, stout-hearted and unclad.

No sooner had the bride arrived than two
    stalwart wrestlers made
    a fierce and ardent display
of muscles, less shielded by scant white linen
    than by their thick dark down.
And so the two of them embraced, and then
—huffing smoke if not perspiring fire—   960
    hindered by mutual knots
as sturdy elms are by entangling vines,
one tenacious ivy to the other's wall.
They are, in short, crafty sons of the earth,[2]
    mighty, if not Alcides,
trying to throw the other down, and thrown,
    like pines rising up rooted
in the deepest bosom of the mountains.
An equal prize honors them. And of four more

---

1 The birds that fly to the Nile.   2 The giant Antaeus, son of Earth, the source of his strength, wrestled Hercules.

ciñe las sienes glorïosa rama,
con que se puso término a la lucha.

Las dos partes rayaba del teatro
el sol, cuando arrogante joven llama
    al expedido salto
la bárbara corona que le escucha.
Arras del animoso desafío
un pardo gabán fué en el verde suelo,
a quien se abaten ocho o diez soberbios
montañeses, cual suele de lo alto
calarse turba de invidiosas aves
a los ojos de Ascálafo, vestido
de perezosas plumas. Quién, de graves
piedras las duras manos impedido,
su agilidad pondera; quién sus nervios
desata estremeciéndose gallardo.
Besó la raya pues el pie desnudo
del suelto mozo, y con airoso vuelo
pisó del viento lo que del ejido
tres veces ocupar pudiera un dardo.

La admiración, vestida un mármol frío,
apenas arquear las cejas pudo;
la emulación, calzada un duro hielo,
torpe se arraiga. Bien que impulso noble
de gloria, aunque villano, solicita
a un vaquero de aquellos montes, grueso,
    membrudo, fuerte roble,
que, ágil a pesar de lo robusto,
al aire se arrebata, violentando
lo grave tanto, que lo precipita

980

990

1000

the brows were circled by the glorious branch,[1]   970
 putting an end to the match.

The sun's rays shone on two thirds of the theater
 when an arrogant youth
 calls for a forward jump
to the rough-hewn circle that can hear him.
The prize for the spirited challenge was
 a dark coat on the greensward,
toward which eight or ten haughty mountain lads
 swoop down, as from on high
a flock of covetous birds tends to tear at   980
 the eyes of Ascalaphus,[2]
 clad in lazy feathers. One,
hard hands burdened by heavy stones, ponders
his agility; another unleashes
 nerves, and quivers gallantly.
Then the bare foot of the graceful youth kissed
 the line, and in weightless flight
trod three times the wind in the pasture that
 a dart perhaps could possess.

Astonishment, accoutered in cold marble,   990
 scarce could raise its eyebrows;
emulation, shod in hard ice, is rooted, slow.[3]
Until a noble impetus toward glory
 solicits, though a peasant,
 a cowherd from those mountains,
 an oak, brawny, stout, and strong,
who, agile in spite of his robust frame,
leaps into air, doing so much violence
 to heft that he is hurled

---

1 That is, the wreath of victory.   2 Ascalaphus was turned into an owl by Proserpine after he told Pluto she had eaten while in the underworld, which meant she would still have to spend time there.   3 The spectators are so astonished they cannot even raise their eyebrows, and challengers seem frozen in place.

—Ícaro montañés—su mismo peso,
de la menuda hierba el seno blando
piélago duro hecho a su rüina.

Si no tan corpulento, más adusto
   serrano le sucede,
   que iguala y aun excede
   al ayuno leopardo,
al corcillo travieso, al muflón sardo
que de las rocas trepa a la marina
   sin dejar ni aun pequeña
del pie ligero bipartida seña.
Con más felicidad que el precedente,
pisó las huellas casi del primero
   el adusto vaquero.
Pasos otro dió al aire, al suelo coces.

Y premïados graduadamente,
advocaron a sí toda la gente
—cierzos del llano y austros de la sierra—
   mancebos tan veloces,
que cuando Ceres más dora la tierra,
y argenta el mar desde sus grutas hondas
   Neptuno, sin fatiga
   su vago pie de pluma
surcar pudiera mieses, pisar ondas,
   sin inclinar espiga,
   sin vïolar espuma.

Dos veces eran diez, y dirigidos
a dos olmos que quieren, abrazados,
ser palios verdes, ser frondosas metas,
   salen cual de torcidos
arcos, o nervïosos o acerados,
con silbo igual, dos veces diez saetas.

1010

1020

1030

1040

—mountain Icarus—headlong by his own weight,   *1000*
and the gentle bosom of common grass
becomes the stony ocean of his ruin.

If not as corpulent, then more austere
    the mountain lad who follows
    and equals, even exceeds
    the hungering leopard,
the racing steed, the wild Sardinian sheep
    that climbs rocks down to the shore
    and leaves behind not the least
    trace of its fleet cloven hoof.   *1010*
More happily than the one who came before,
    the austere cowherd nearly
    trod the footprints of the first.
Another stepped on the air, kicked at the earth.

    And when they were awarded
according to their deserts, then all the people
—north winds of the plain, south winds of the mountains—
    heed striplings so light-footed
that when Ceres turns the earth most golden
and from his deepest grottoes Neptune silvers   *1020*
    the sea, then tirelessly
    their wandering feathered feet
could cut a wake through grains, could tread on waves,
    without bending over a stalk,
    without profaning the foam.[1]

    Twice ten they were, moving toward
    two elms embraced that wish
to be green trophies, leafy finish lines,
    as if from twisted bows
    of nerves or steel were shot,   *1030*
with an identical hiss, arrows twice ten.

1 A group assembles for a race, so swift they seem to have wings on their feet.

No el polvo desparece
el campo, que no pisan alas hierba;
es el más torpe una herida cierva,
el más tardo la vista desvanece,
y, siguiendo al más lento,
    cojea el pensamiento.

El tercio casi de una milla era
    la prolija carrera
que los hercúleos troncos hace breves;
    pero las plantas leves
    de tres sueltos zagales
la distancia sincopan tan iguales,
que la atención confunden judiciosa.

De la Peneida virgen desdeñosa,
los dulces fugitivos miembros bellos
en la corteza no abrazó, reciente,
más firme Apolo, más estrechamente,
que de una y otra meta glorïosa
las duras basas abrazaron ellos
    con triplicado nudo.
Árbitro Alcides en sus ramas, dudo
    que el caso decidiera,
bien que su menor hoja un ojo fuera
    del lince más agudo.

En tanto pues que el palio neutro pende
y la carroza de la luz desciende
a templarse en las ondas, Himeneo
—por templar, en los brazos, el deseo
del galán novio, de la esposa bella—
los rayos anticipa de la estrella,
cerúlea ahora, ya purpúrea guía
de los dudosos términos del día.

Dust does not cause the field
to disappear, for wings do not tread on grass;
   the slowest a wounded doe,
   the most laggard makes sight reel,
and tracking the most sluggish renders thought lame.

   Near the third part of a mile
   was the length of the course
that makes the trunks of Hercules[1] seem small;
   but the swiftly moving feet   1040
   of three loose-limbed peasant lads
overcome the distance in so like a guise
that the verdict of the judges is confused.

Apollo did not embrace more closely,
more firmly, the fleeing members, lovely, sweet,
of the disdainful Peneian virgin
   newly transformed into bark[2]
   than they the unyielding bases
   in a triparted knot.
If Alcides in their branches were a judge   1050
   I doubt he could decide,
   even if their least leaf
transmuted into the lynx's sharpest eye.

As the neutral trophy waits, undecided,
and the chariot of the light descends
   to cool in the waves, Hymen
—to cool, in the other's arms, the desire
of the gallant groom, the beautiful bride—
   waits for the rays of the star,[3]
   now azure, then purple guide   1060
to the nebulous limits of the day.

---

1 The elms, sacred to Hercules, that serve as the finish line seem distant. 2 Daphne, daughter of the river god Peneus, was pursued by Apollo, but was transformed into a laurel before he could reach her. 3 Venus, both morning and evening star.

El jüicio—al de todos, indeciso—
    del concurso ligero,
el padrino con tres de limpio acero
cuchillos corvos absolvello quiso.
Solícita Junón, Amor no omiso,
al son de otra zampoña que conduce
ninfas bellas y sátiros lascivos,
los desposados a su casa vuelven,
    que coronada luce
de estrellas fijas, de astros fugitivos
que en sonoroso humo se resuelven.

Llegó todo el lugar, y, despedido,
casta Venus—que el lecho ha prevenido
de las plumas que baten más süaves
en su volante carro blancas aves—
los novios entra en dura no estacada:
que, siendo Amor una deidad alada,
bien previno la hija de la espuma
a batallas de amor campo de pluma.

The outcome—undecided
in the opinion of all—of the footrace
the patron of the wedding wished to resolve
    with three curved knives of clean steel.[1]
Solicitous Juno, attentive Love,[2]
to the sound of other panpipes led by
beautiful nymphs and lascivious satyrs,
    lead the couple to their house
    crowned by fixed and falling stars   *1070*
    that resolve in sounding smoke.

The entire village arrived, then took their leave,
and chaste Venus—who prepared the bed
with the feathers the white birds of her flying
    carriage beat most gently[3]—
brings bride and groom onto the field, not hard:
    for Love, being a winged god,
the daughter of the foam prepared a field
of swan feathers for the battles of love.

1 The wedding's sponsor rewards each runner with a knife.   2 The gods that preside over weddings.   3 Venus's chariot is drawn by swans. Here she is the goddess of married love.

SOLEDAD
SEGUNDA

Éntrase el mar por un arroyo breve
que a recibillo con sediento paso
de su roca natal se precipita,
y mucha sal no sólo en poco vaso,
    mas su rüina bebe,
y su fin, cristalina mariposa
    —no alada, sino undosa—,
en el farol de Tetis solicita.

Muros desmantelando, pues, de arena,
centauro ya espumoso el Ocëano
    —medio mar, medio ría—
dos veces huella la campaña al día,
escalar pretendiendo el monte en vano,
    de quien es dulce vena
    el tarde ya torrente
arrepentido, y aun retrocediente.

Eral lozano así novillo tierno,
    de bien nacido cuerno
    mal lunada la frente,
retrógrado cedió en desigual lucha
a duro toro, aun contra el viento armado:
    no pues de otra manera

THE SECOND
SOLITUDE

The ocean flows into a narrow brook
that, to receive it, with a thirsting pace
rushes impetuous from its natal rock,
quaffs from a small cup quantities of salt
    along with its own ruin,
    its end—butterfly of crystal
    not wingéd but well waved—
solicited in Thetis's great lamp.[1]

And, demolishing ramparts made of sand,
Ocean a centaur—half ria, half sea—   10
    a beast of foaming spume
marauds the land twice each day,
attempting in vain to scale the palisade
    down which the narrow brook,
    a late-repentant torrent,
ever receding, is now a gentle stream.

Just as the antic calf, high-spirited, young,
    its forehead barely half-mooned
    with well-formed maturing horns,
retreated, ceded in unequal battle   20
to the fierce bull, armed even against the wind:
    in this way and no other

---

1 One of the Nereids, minor marine deities; the sea is imaged as her lamp.

a la violencia mucha
del padre de las aguas, coronado
de blancas ovas y de espuma verde,
resiste obedeciendo, y tierra pierde.

En la incierta ribera
—guarnición desigual a tanto espejo—,
descubrió la alba a nuestro peregrino
con todo el villanaje ultramarino,
que a la fiesta nupcial, de verde tejo
toldado, ya capaz tradujo pino.

Los escollos el sol rayaba, cuando,
con remos gemidores,
dos pobres se aparecen pescadores,
nudos al mar de cáñamo fiando.
Ruiseñor en los bosques no más blando,
el verde robre que es barquillo ahora,
saludar vió la Aurora,
que al uno en dulces quejas—y no pocas—
ondas endurecer, liquidar rocas.

Señas mudas la dulce voz doliente
permitió solamente
a la turba, que dar quisiera voces
a la que de un ancón segunda haya
—cristal pisando azul con pies veloces—
salió improvisa, de una y otra playa
vínculo desatado, instable puente.

La prora diligente
no sólo dirigió a la opuesta orilla,
mas redujo la música barquilla,
que en dos cuernos del mar caló no breves
sus plomos graves y sus corchos leves.

does it resist, obeying and losing ground
    to the immense violence
    of the father of waters,
crowned in white algae, wreathéd in green foam.

    On the inconstant seacoast
—a rough-hewn frame to so large a mirror—
    dawn discovered our pilgrim
with all the villagers from the other shore   *30*
who, to the wedding feast, shaded by a green
canopy, were carried in a worthy craft.

On the reefs the rays of the sun were shining when
    with a groaning of the oars
    two poor fishermen appeared,
entrusting their knotted hemp net to the sea.
The green oak that is now their little bark
ne'er heard a nightingale greet more tenderly
    Aurora in the woods
than the one whose sweet laments—and not a few—   *40*
now turn the waves to stone, to water the rocks.

Unspoken signs were all that gentle sad voice
would permit the villagers who wished to hail
    a second bark that emerged
    unforeseen from a cove,
—treading blue crystal with swift-moving feet[1]—
unmoored link, unstable bridge between two shores.

    Its prow, untiring, intent,
    moved toward the opposite shore,
bringing with it the melodious bark   *50*
that in two horns, not small, of the sea, let down
    heavy lead weights and light corks.[2]

---

[1] The image evokes the oars of the boat.   [2] That is, the fisherman who was
singing casts his nets.

Los senos ocupó del mayor leño
  la marítima tropa,
  usando al entrar todos
cuantos les enseñó corteses modos
en la lengua del agua ruda escuela,
con nuestro forastero, que la popa
del canoro escogió bajel pequeño.

Aquél, las ondas escarchando, vuela;
éste, con perezoso movimiento,
el mar encuentra, cuya espuma cana
  su parda aguda prora
  resplandeciente cuello
hace de augusta Coya peruana,
a quien hilos el Sur tributó ciento
  de perlas cada hora.
Lágrimas no enjugó más de la Aurora
sobre víolas negras la mañana,
que arrolló su espolón con pompa vana
caduco aljófar, pero aljófar bello.

Dando el huésped licencia para ello,
recurren no a las redes que, mayores,
mucho Océano y pocas aguas prenden,
sino a las que ambiciosas menos penden,
laberinto nudoso de marino
Dédalo, si de leño no, de lino,
fábrica escrupulosa, y aunque incierta,
siempre murada, pero siempre abierta.

Liberalmente de los pescadores
al deseo el estero corresponde,
sin valelle al lascivo ostión el justo

The crowd of mariners
took over the bosom of the larger craft,
    using as they climbed aboard
    all the courtesies and words
taught them in the rustic school of the sea
with our stranger, who for himself chose the stern
    of the small musical boat.

The first flies, frosting the waves;   60
the second, in an indolent motion meets
    the sea, whose white-colored foam
    makes of its dark slender prow
    the bright resplendent throat
of an august Coya, empress of Peru,[1]
to whom the Southern Sea[2] rendered each hour
    one hundred strands of pearls.
The morning dried no more of Aurora's tears
    shed on black violets
than the pearls, fleeting but beautiful pearls   70
    overridden and crushed by
    the cutwater in vain show.

Their guest giving his leave,
they turn not to the larger nets that capture
    abundant Ocean and a dearth of water
    but less ambitious ones that hang,
the knotted labyrinths of a maritime
Daedalus,[3] of linen if not of wood,
scrupulously made, and although mutable
    a wall, but always open.   80

Most liberally does the inlet respond
    to the fishermen's wishes,
    not freeing the lustful oyster from the tight

---

1 Among the Incas, the wife of the emperor, or Inca, was called Coya.
2 The Southern Sea is the Pacific Ocean.   3 The architect of the labyrinth
that housed (and hid) the Minotaur, who was half man, half bull.

arnés de hueso, donde
lisonja breve al gusto
—mas incentiva—esconde:
contagio original quizá de aquella
que, siempre hija bella
de los cristales, una
90   venera fué su cuna.

Mallas visten de cáñamo al lenguado,
mientras, en su piel lúbrica fiado,
el congrio, que viscosamente liso,
    las telas burlar quiso,
tejido en ellas se quedó burlado.

Las redes califica menos gruesas,
    sin romper hilo alguno,
pompa el salmón de las reales mesas,
cuando no de los campos de Neptuno,
100   y el travieso robalo,
guloso de los Cónsules regalo.

Estos y muchos más, unos desnudos,
otros de escamas fáciles armados,
    dió la ría pescados,
que, nadando en un piélago de nudos,
no agravan poco el negligente robre,
espacïosamente dirigido
al bienaventurado albergue pobre,
que, de carrizos frágiles tejido,
110   si fabricado no de gruesas cañas,
bóvedas lo coronan de espadañas.

El peregrino, pues, haciendo en tanto
instrumento el bajel, cuerdas los remos,
al céfiro encomienda los extremos
    deste métrico llanto:

harness of shell, where it hides
a small—but goading—desire:
original contagion perhaps of one
who, ever the beautiful
daughter of crystal, had for
a cradle a scallop shell.[1]

Meshes of hemp clothe the sole   90
while, trusting to its slippery oiled skin,
the conger eel, viscous, smooth,
wished to deceive the webs,
but, intertwined in them, was deceived instead.

Finer nets are ennobled
with none of their cords broken
by the salmon, splendor of royal tables,
if not of the fields of Neptune,
and the mischievous sea bass,
epicurean gift of Consuls of Rome.   100

These fish and many others,
bare or armed with pliant scales
were offered by the ria,
and swimming in a sea of knots,
they do not weigh lightly in the laggard bark
slow-moving toward the poor and simple shelter
that, woven of fragile reeds
or constructed of stout cane,
is crowned by vaults of cattails.

And meanwhile the pilgrim, making of the craft   110
an instrument, turning its oars into strings,
commends to the breeze extremes
of this poetic lament:

1 The oyster is said to arouse erotic desire in those who eat it, perhaps through
the influence of Venus, "daughter of crystal"—that is, of the ocean's water.

«Si de aire articulado
no son dolientes lágrimas süaves
 estas mis quejas graves,
voces de sangre, y sangre son del alma.
 Fíelas de tu calma,
¡oh mar!, quien otra vez las ha fiado
de tu fortuna aún más que de su hado.

 ¡Oh mar, oh tú, supremo
moderador piadoso de mis daños!:
 tuyos serán mis años,
en tabla redimidos poco fuerte,
 de la bebida muerte,
que ser quiso, en aquel peligro extremo,
ella el forzado y su guadaña el remo.

 Regiones pise ajenas,
o clima propio, planta mía perdida,
 tuya será mi vida,
sï vida me ha dejado que sea tuya
 quien me fuerza a que huya
de su prisión, dejando mis cadenas
rastro en tus ondas más que en tus arenas.

 Audaz mi pensamiento
el cenit escaló, plumas vestido,
 cuyo vuelo atrevido
—si no ha dado su nombre a tus espumas—
 de sus vestidas plumas
conservarán el desvanecimiento
los anales diáfanos del viento.

 Esta, pues, culpa mía
el timón alternar menos seguro
 y el báculo más duro

"If these my solemn plaints
are not the delicate, sorrowful tears
   of articulated breath,
they are the words of blood, blood of my soul.
   He may trust them to thy calm,
oh sea! who trusted them another time
to thy tempest even more than to his fate.   *120*

   Oh sea, oh thou, supreme
assuager, merciful to my sorrows!
   thine will be my years
   redeemed on a fragile plank
   from a watery death,
who chose to be, in that utmost of dangers,
thyself the galley slave, and thy scythe the oar.

Whether my wandering steps tread foreign climes
   or walk on native soil
   my life will always be thine,   *130*
if any life is left to me to give thee
   by one who forced me to flee
her prison, my chains leaving behind a trail
   on thy waves, not on thy sands.

   With audacity my thought
   scaled the heights, clad in feathers,
   whose daring incautious flight[1]
—if it has not given thy foam its name—
   of its well-feathered raiment
the diaphanous annals of the wind   *140*
   will preserve the vanishment.

This fault of mine, then, for a lustrum has moved
my indecisive hand back and forth between
   the least secure rudder and

---

1 The figure of Icarus is evoked here.

un lustro ha hecho a mi dudosa mano,
   solicitando en vano
las alas sepultar de mi osadía
150   donde el sol nace o donde muere el día.

   Muera, enemiga amada,
muera mi culpa, y tu desdén le guarde,
   arrepentido tarde,
suspiro que mi muerte haga leda,
   cuando no le suceda,
o por breve o por tibia o por cansada,
lágrima antes enjuta que llorada.

   Naufragio ya segundo,
o filos pongan de homicida hierro
160   fin duro a mi destierro;
tan generosa fe, no fácil onda,
   no poca tierra esconda:
urna suya el Océano profundo,
y obeliscos los montes sean del mundo.

   Túmulo tanto debe
agradecido Amor a mi pie errante;
   líquido, pues, diamante
calle mis huesos, y elevada cima
   selle sí, mas no oprima,
170   esta que le fiaré ceniza breve,
si hay ondas mudas y si hay tierra leve.»

No es sordo el mar: la erudición engaña.
   Bien que tal vez sañudo
no oya al piloto, o le responda fiero,
sereno disimula más orejas
   que sembró dulces quejas
—canoro labrador—el forastero
   en su undosa campaña.

the most arduous staff,
ever attempting in vain
to bury the wings of my audacity[1]
where the sun is born or where day goes to die.

Die, beloved enemy,
let my fault die, and your disdain, too late   150
    a penitent, keep for it
a mere sigh that makes my death content
    though it is not followed by
a fleeting or indifferent or weary
tear that dries before it is even wept.

Whether a second shipwreck
or the sharp edges of murderous steel put
    to my exile a cruel end;
no trifling wave, no handful of earth can hide
    faith as generous as mine: 160
    deepest Ocean be its urn
and mountains of the world its obelisks.

So great a burial mound
a grateful Love owes to my wandering feet;
then let diamond liquid conceal my bones,
    high peaks seal but not oppress
    these few ashes I entrust to them
if there are silent waves and lightweight earth."

The sea is not deaf: erudition deceives.
    Though perhaps when in a rage   170
it may not hear the pilot or respond with
fury, when serene it pardons more ears
    than the sweet laments sown by
—a lyrical farmer—the pilgrim stranger
    in its vast field of waves.

1 That is, the audacity of thinking his love would be reciprocated by his
"beloved enemy."

Espongïoso, pues, se bebió y mudo
180 el lagrimoso reconocimiento,
de cuyos dulces números no poca
   concentuosa suma
en los dos giros de invisible pluma
que fingen sus dos alas, hurtó el viento;
Eco—vestida una cavada roca—
solicitó curiosa y guardó avara
la más dulce—si no la menos clara—
   sílaba, siendo en tanto
la vista de las chozas fin del canto.

190 Yace en el mar, si no continuada,
isla mal de la tierra dividida,
cuya forma tortuga es perezosa:
díganlo cuantos siglos ha que nada
sin besar de la playa espacïosa
la arena, de las ondas repetida.

A pesar, pues, del agua que la oculta,
concha, si mucha no, capaz ostenta
de albergues, donde la humildad contenta
mora, y Pomona se venera culta.

200 Dos son las chozas, pobre su artificio
más aún que caduca su materia:
de los mancebos dos, la mayor, cuna:
de las redes la otra y su ejercicio,
   competente oficina.
Lo que agradable más se determina
del breve islote, ocupa su fortuna,

And so, like a sponge, and mute, the sea drank up
   his tearful gratitude,
   of whose sweet ciphers a sum
   not small of harmony
in two turns of invisible feathers feigned   *180*
by its two wings was stolen by the wind;
Echo—clad in deep-carved rock[1]—
with curiosity requested and with
   avarice kept the sweetest
—if not the least clear—syllable, while the sight
   of the huts ended the plaint.

In the sea there lies, if not continuous
with the mainland, an island barely separate
from it, shaped like an indolent tortoise:
let the many centuries it has been   *190*
swimming without planting a kiss on the sand
   of the broad beach speak to this,
   though waves oft have brushed the coast.

And so, no matter the water that hides it,
the shell, not large, but large enough to reveal
the shelters where a humble contentment dwells
and pays its homage to Pomona's cult.[2]

Two huts, their contrivance even poorer
than their material is old and frail:
the larger the cradle of the two young men,   *200*
   the other a fit storeroom
for nets and other devices of their trade.
Of the rest of the small island, the most
   pleasant portion is theirs,

1 A nymph punished by Juno, who turned her into a mere duplicative sound—that is, an echo. 2 Pomona was a divinity of fruit orchards.

los extremos de fausto y de miseria
moderando.

        En la plancha los recibe
el padre de los dos, émulo cano
del sagrado Nereo, no ya tanto
porque a la par de los escollos vive,
porque en el mar preside comarcano
al ejercicio piscatorio, cuanto
por seis hijas, por seis deidades bellas,
del cielo espumas y del mar estrellas.

Acogió al huésped con urbano estilo,
y a su voz, que los juncos obedecen,
tres hijas suyas cándidas le ofrecen,
que engaños construyendo, están de hilo.
El huerto le da esotras, a quien debe
si púrpura la rosa, el lilio nieve.

De jardín culto así en fingida gruta,
salteó al labrador pluvia improvisa
de cristales inciertos, a la seña,
o a la que torció llave el fontanero:
urna de Acuario, la imitada peña
lo embiste incauto, y si con pie grosero
para la fuga apela, nubes pisa,
burlándolo aun la parte más enjuta.

La vista saltearon poco menos
    del huésped admirado
las no líquidas perlas, que, al momento,
a los corteses juncos—porque el viento

moderating extremes of grandeur and
indigence.

      At the gangplank they are welcomed
by the father of the two, white-haired mirror
of the sacred Nereus,[1] less because he
    lives near reefs, or fishing rules   210
    in nearby seas, than because
of six daughters, six beautiful goddesses,
foam of the heavens and stars of the sea.[2]

With courteous manners he welcomed the guest,
and at his call, which the bulrushes obey,
three guileless daughters, weaving nets of hempen
    strands, appear before them.
The garden presents the others, to whom
the rose owes its scarlet, the lily its snow.

From a feigned grotto in the tended garden   220
unforeseen rain of vacillant crystals
waylaid the rustic at a sign or tap turned
    by the fountain-keeper:
pitcher of Aquarius,[3] the false crag
assails the unwary man, and if confused
    feet turn to flight, they tread clouds,
even the most arid ground is mocking him.

Only slightly less were the eyes of the
    dumbfounded guest astonished
by the not liquid pearls who, for the moment,   230
    remit the well-knotted hemp

1 A sea divinity and father of the fifty Nereids, the nymphs of the sea. 2 In
comparing the six daughters to goddesses, certain attributes of Venus are
merged in the image: she was born in the ocean foam and is the morning and
evening star. 3 Aquarius, the water bearer, is usually depicted as holding a
pitcher of water.

nudos les halle un día, bien que ajenos—
el cáñamo remiten anudado,
y de Vertumno al término labrado
el breve hierro, cuyo corvo diente
las plantas le mordía cultamente.

Ponderador saluda afectuoso
del esplendor que admira el extranjero
al Sol, en seis luceros dividido;
y—honestamente al fin correspondido
    del coro vergonzoso—
al viejo sigue, que prudente ordena
los términos confunda de la cena
la comida prolija de pescados,
raros muchos, y todos no comprados.

Impidiéndole el día al forastero,
con dilaciones sordas le divierte
entre unos verdes carrizales, donde
armonïoso número se esconde
de blancos cisnes, de la misma suerte
que gallinas domésticas al grano,
a la voz concurrientes del anciano.

En la más seca, en la más limpia anea
vivificando están muchos sus huevos,
y mientras dulce aquél su muerte anuncia
    entre la verde juncia,
sus pollos éste al mar conduce nuevos,
    de Espío y de Nerea
—cuando más obscurecen las espumas—
nevada invidia, sus nevadas plumas.

240

250

260

to the courteous rushes—so that the wind
can find knots, though not their own, in them one day—
and the small metal blade on the tilled domain
    of Vertumnus,[1] its curved tooth
    biting plants as it plowed them.[2]

Pondering the splendor that amazes him
with affection the stranger greets the Sun
    cleaved into six morning stars;
and—answered at last so modestly by the
    shy and diffident chorus—
follows the old man, who prudently orders
    an abundant meal of fish
    many rare, not one purchased,
that confounds the boundaries of supper.

    Filling the stranger's day,
    with mute delays he keeps him
    among green fields of reeds
where an affectionate bevy of white swans
is hiding, and as domestic hens gather
for grain, they come when the ancient man calls.

On the driest bulrushes and the cleanest,
    many give life to their eggs,
and as one sweetly announces her own death[3]
    among the green-hued sedge,
another leads to the sea her newborn chicks,
their snowy plumage the pure white envy
    of Espion and Nereis[4]
    —who make sea foam seem dark.

240

250

1 A Roman deity associated with the transformation of plants from blossom to fruit. 2 The "not liquid pearls" are the six daughters, three of whom leave their nets in the rushes, while the other three put down their farming implements. 3 Swans were supposed to sing just before they died. In other words, this was her swan song. 4 Nymphs whose skin was so white it made "sea foam seem dark."

Hermana de Faetón, verde el cabello,
les ofrece el que, joven ya gallardo,
de flexuosas mimbres garbín pardo
tosco le ha encordonado, pero bello.
Lo más liso trepó, lo más sublime
venció su agilidad, y artificiosa
tejió en sus ramas inconstantes nidos
donde celosa arrulla y ronca gime
la ave lasciva de la cipria diosa.
Mástiles coronó menos crecidos,
gavia no tan capaz: extraño todo,
el designio, la fábrica y el modo.

A pocos pasos le admiró no menos
montecillo, las sienes laureado,
traviesos despidiendo moradores
    de sus confusos senos,
conejuelos, que—el viento consultado—
salieron retozando a pisar flores:
el más tímido, al fin, más ignorante
    del plomo fulminante.

Cóncavo fresno—a quien gracioso indulto
de su caduco natural permite
que a la encina vivaz robusto imite,
y hueco exceda al alcornoque inculto—
verde era pompa de un vallete oculto,
cuando frondoso alcázar no, de aquella,
que sin corona vuela y sin espada,
susurrante amazona, Dido alada,
de ejército más casto, de más bella

Phaethon's sister[1] is revealed   260
by one who, when he was nimble and young
laced a net coif, rough, dark-hued, but comely
of pliant ozier in her leaf-green hair.
He climbed the smoothest bark, the loftiest
vanquished by agility, artfully wove
    in her branches changeful nests
where jealous coo and throaty moan the wanton
birds of the goddess of the Cyprian isle.[2]
Crow's nests less ample crowned masts not as high:
all of it strange, design and structure and style.   270

A few paces past he was no less surprised
by a hill, its temples wreathed in laurel,
where roguish rabbits leaving their burrows
    in its intricate bosom
    —having consulted the wind—
come out to gambol among the flowers:
the most timid, after all, most ignorant
    of fulminating lead.

A concave ash tree—a gracious clemency
    of its frail nature allows   280
it to imitate the hale longevity
of the oak, and hollow to exceed the rough
cork—green pomp was of a hidden glen
    if not the leafy fortress
of she who flies without a crown or sword,
murmuring Amazon, a wingéd Dido[3]
of the most chaste army, the republic

---

1 Phaethon drove the Sun's chariot across the sky, lost control of the horses, and almost burned the earth. Jupiter killed him as punishment and turned his sisters, who had helped him, into poplar trees. 2 Doves are sacred to Venus, "goddess of the Cyprian isle." 3 Dido was the queen of Carthage; the Amazons were female warriors ruled by their queen, Penthesilea. The queen bee is compared to both monarchs.

república, ceñida, en vez de muros,
de cortezas; en esta, pues, Cartago
reina la abeja, oro brillando vago,
o el jugo beba de los aires puros,
o el sudor de los cielos, cuando liba
de las mudas estrellas la saliva;
burgo eran suyo el tronco informe, el breve
corcho, y moradas pobres sus vacíos,
300   del que más solicita los desvíos
de la isla, plebeyo enjambre leve.

Llegaron luego donde al mar se atreve,
si promontorio no, un cerro elevado,
   de cabras estrellado,
   iguales, aunque pocas,
a la que—imagen décima del cielo—
flores su cuerno es, rayos su pelo.

«Éstas», dijo el isleño venerable,
«y aquéllas que, pendientes de las rocas,
310   tres o cuatro desean para ciento,
—redil las ondas y pastor el viento—
libres discurren, su nocivo diente
paz hecha con las plantas inviolable.»

Estimando seguía el peregrino
   al venerable isleño,
de muchos pocos numeroso dueño,
cuando los suyos enfrenó de un pino
el pie villano, que groseramente
los cristales pisaba de una fuente.

320   Ella, pues, sierpe, y sierpe al fin pisada,
—aljófar vomitando fugitivo
   en lugar de veneno—

most fair, girded not by walls but by bark;
    in this Carthage, then, the queen
    bee reigns, vagrant gold flying,   290
drinking in the elixir of pure air
or beads of perspiration from the sky
when she sips the saliva of mute stars;[1]
her city the ill-formed trunk, the small cork,
    their hollows the poor dwellings
    of the swift plebeian swarm
that seeks out the hidden places on the isle.

Then they came to where the sea is challenged by
if not a promontory then a high hill
    studded and starred with she-goats,   300
    just like the one, though fewer,
    —tenth image in the heavens—
whose horn is flowers, whose coat is made of beams.[2]

"These," the venerable islander said,
    "and those, pendant from the rocks,
    three or four shy of a hundred,
—their goat pen the waves, their goatherd the wind—
    wander free, their harmful teeth
having declared a sacred peace with our crops."

    The pilgrim, honoring him,   310
followed after the venerable islander,
    master of many small realms,
when his were halted by the rustic foot
    of a pine that rudely trod
    the crystals of a fountain.

A serpent, after all, a trodden serpent
    —spewing short-lived pearls instead of poison—

---

1 That is, the dew. 2 Amalthea, the goat that nursed Jupiter, represented
in the constellation Capricorn, the tenth sign of the zodiac. Her horn was
transformed into the horn of plenty, or Cornucopia.

torcida esconde, ya que no enroscada,
las flores, que de un parto dió lascivo
aura fecunda al matizado seno
del huerto, en cuyos troncos se desata
de las escamas que vistió de plata.

Seis chopos, de seis yedras abrazados,
tirsos eran del griego dios, nacido
330   segunda vez, que en pámpanos desmiente
    los cuernos de su frente;
y cual mancebos tejen anudados
festivos corros en alegre ejido,
coronan ellos el encanecido
suelo de lilios, que en fragantes copos
nevó el mayo, a pesar de los seis chopos.

Este sitio las bellas seis hermanas
    escogen, agraviando
en breve espacio mucha primavera
340   con las mesas, cortezas ya livianas
del árbol que ofreció a la edad primera
duro alimento, pero sueño blando.

Nieve hilada, y por sus manos bellas
caseramente a telas reducida,
    manteles blancos fueron.
Sentados, pues, sin ceremonias, ellas
en torneado fresno la comida
    con silencio sirvieron.

Rompida el agua en las menudas piedras,
350   cristalina sonante era tiorba,

twisting and hiding, when it is not coiled,[1]
the flowers that fecund dawn joyously birthed
in the shaded bosom of the orchard   320
    among whose trunks it lets go
    of the silver scales it wore.

Six black poplars embraced by six ivy vines,
    thyrsi were to the twice-born
    Greek god,[2] who hides with tendrils
    the horns growing on his brow;
    and like striplings linked who weave
festive circles in a joyful meadow,
they crown with lilies the ground, turning it white
with fragrant flakes of snow that May let fall   330
    in spite of the six poplars.

    This spot the six fair sisters
    have chosen, violating
in a small space a large portion of spring
    with their tables, the light bark
of the tree that offered to the golden age
    hard sustenance but soft sleep.[3]

    Snow spun and by lovely hands
    converted at home to cloth
    and spread white on the tables.   340
When all were seated, without formalities,
silently the sisters served the food in
    vessels of well-turned ash.

    Water breaking on small stones
was of a theorbo[4] the sound crystalline,

---

1 The stream is compared to a snake winding among the trees. 2 The
thyrsus is the wand carried by Bacchus, removed from his mother's womb
and placed in the thigh of his father, Jupiter, until he came to term. 3 The
cork tree, source of acorns for food and soft bark for beds. 4 A double-
necked lute with two sets of strings.

y las confusamente acordes aves,
entre las verdes roscas de las yedras,
muchas eran, y muchas veces nueve
aladas musas, que—de pluma leve
engañada su oculta lira corva—
metros inciertos sí, pero süaves,
en idïomas cantan diferentes;
mientras, cenando en pórfidos lucientes,
    lisonjean apenas
360   al Júpiter marino tres sirenas.

Comieron, pues, y rudamente dadas
gracias el pescador a la divina
próvida mano, «¡Oh bien vividos años!
¡Oh canas», dijo el huésped, «no peinadas
con boj dentado o con rayada espina,
sino con verdaderos desengaños!
Pisad dichoso esta esmeralda bruta,
en mármol engastada siempre undoso,
jubilando la red en los que os restan
370   felices años, y la humedecida
    o poco rato enjuta
próxima arena de esa opuesta playa,
    la remota Cambaya
sea de hoy más a vuestro leño ocioso;
y el mar que os la divide, cuanto cuestan
    Océano importuno
a las Quinas—del viento aun veneradas—
    sus ardientes veneros,
su esfera lapidosa de luceros.

380   Del pobre albergue a la barquilla pobre,
geómetra prudente, el orbe mida
    vuestra planta, impedida

and myriad birds among the ivy coils
sang in a confusion of harmonies,
many times nine wingéd muses—light feathers
   conceal the hidden curved lyre—
that in meters uncertain but very sweet   *350*
   sing in diverse idioms;
meanwhile, dining on gleaming porphyries,
   three sirens do not offer
as much delight to the ocean's Jupiter.[1]

And so they ate, and the fisherman having
offered unschooled thanks to the providential
   hand divine, "Oh years well lived!
   Oh white hair!" said the guest,
"Not combed with dentate boxwood or grooved thorn
but with true clear-sightedness!   *360*
Tread in good fortune this emerald animal,[2]
   set in marble ever waved,
retire your nets in your remaining contented
   years, and let the ever damp
   or only briefly dry
sand of that nearby beach on terra firma
   be from now on far Cambay[3]
to your idle bark; and the sea that divides
you all that importunate Ocean demands
   of Portugal's coat-of-arms   *370*
   —venerated by the wind—
   for her ardent veins and lodes,
her lapidary sphere of brilliant stars.[4]

From poor hut to fishing boat just as poor,
like a prudent geometer, let your foot
   measure the world, impeded

---

1 The sirens were sea nymphs whose song had the power to charm; the
"ocean's Jupiter" is Neptune. 2 That is, the tortoise-shaped island sur-
rounded by waves. 3 A state and city in India. 4 The precious stones
Portugal obtained from her Asian colonies.

—si de purpúreas conchas, no, istriadas—
de trágicas rüinas de alto robre,
que—el tridente acusando de Neptuno—
  menos quizá dió astillas
que ejemplos de dolor a estas orillas.»

«Días ha muchos, oh mancebo», dijo
  el pescador anciano,
«que en el uno cedí y el otro hermano
el duro remo, el cáñamo prolijo;
  muchos ha dulces días
que cisnes me recuerdan a la hora
  que huyendo la Aurora
las canas de Titón, halla las mías,
a pesar de mi edad, no en la alta cumbre
de aquel morro difícil, cuyas rocas
tarde o nunca pisaron cabras pocas,
y milano venció con pesadumbre,
sino desotro escollo al mar pendiente;
de donde ese teatro de Fortuna
descubro, ese voraz, ese profundo
campo ya de sepulcros, que, sediento,
cuanto, en vasos de abeto, Nuevo Mundo
—tributos digo américos—se bebe
en túmulos de espuma paga breve.

Bárbaro observador, mas diligente,
de las inciertas formas de la Luna,
a cada conjunción su pesquería,
y a cada pesquería su instrumento

390

400

410

—if not by striate then by purple shells—
by tragic ruins of the tall stout oak that
　—warning of Neptune's trident—
　perhaps gave fewer fragments   380
than examples of sorrow to these shores."[1]

　"It has been a while, my boy,"
　the ancient fisherman said,
"since I handed over to both my sons
　the harsh oars and lengthy hemp;
　for many sweet days now swans
　waken me at the hour that
Aurora, fleeing white hair of Tithonus,[2]
discovers mine, in spite of my age, awake,
not on the high peak of that toilsome highland   390
　whose rocks few goats ever trod,
goshawks vanquished only with tribulation,
but on that other reef rising from the sea;
　there I watch Fortune's theater,[3]
　the voracious, the profound
　graveyard thirstily drinking
from goblets of fir all that the New World
—I mean the tributes from the Americas—
pays in mausoleums of short-lived spume.

An observer not learned but diligent   400
　of Luna's changeable forms,[4]
to each conjunction a kind of fishing,
to each kind of fishing its own implements

---

1 The pilgrim pleads with the old fisherman to stay home, even if he does not find pearls in striated shells, taking shipwrecks as a warning against the dangers of Neptune's trident, that is, of going to sea.　2 A sea deity granted immortality at the request of Aurora, or Dawn, who loved him, but he was not granted eternal youth at the same time. The ocean foam is imagined as his white hair.　3 That is, the ocean that brings treasure from the Americas and serves as a cemetery for the ships and men lost in the process.　4 Luna is the moon, "changeable" because of its phases. A "conjunction" refers to the new moon.

—más o menos nudoso—atribuído,
mis hijos dos en un batel despido,
que, el mar cribando en redes no comunes,
vieras intempestivos algún día
—entre un vulgo nadante, digno apenas
de escama, cuanto más de nombre—atunes
vomitar ondas y azotar arenas.

Tal vez desde los muros destas rocas
    cazar a Tetis veo
420   y pescar a Diana en dos barquillas:
náuticas venatorias maravillas
de mis hijas oirás, ambiguo coro,
menos de aljaba que de red armado,
    de cuyo, si no alado,
harpón vibrante, supo mal Proteo
en globos de agua redimir sus focas.

Torpe la más veloz, marino toro,
torpe, mas toro al fin, que el mar violado
de la púrpura viendo de sus venas,
430   bufando mide el campo de las ondas
con la animosa cuerda, que prolija
al hierro sigue que en la foca huye,
o grutas ya la privilegien hondas,
o escollos desta isla divididos:
Láquesis nueva mi gallarda hija,
si Cloto no de la escamada fiera,
ya hila, ya devana su carrera,
cuando desatinada pide, o cuando
    vencida restituye
440   los términos de cáñamo pedidos.

—more knots or fewer—accord,
I bid farewell to my two sons in their boat,
who sieve the sea with uncommon nets;
    you should one day see tuna
—among swimming commoners barely worthy
    of having scales, much less names—
spewing waves and lashing sands.   *410*

And perhaps from the ramparts of these rocks
    I can see Thetis hunting
and Diana fishing in two small boats:[1]
about my daughters marvels nautical
and venatic you will hear, a dubious choir:
    armed not with quiver or net,
against whose if not winged then vibrant harpoon
Proteus[2] could not defend his herds of seals
    even in globes of water.

    Slow the swiftest sea bull,   *420*
slow but a bull after all that, the sea
offended by purple spilling from its veins,
    snorts, measures the field of waves
    with the long spirited line
that trails the metal in the fleeing seal,
whether the beast takes refuge in deep grottoes
    or this island's riven reefs:
a new Lachesis my gallant daughter
or Clotho to the wary animal,[3]
as she plays out or reels in the line, its flight,   *430*
when rashly it demands or vanquished restores
the requested limits of the hempen rope.

1 His two daughters are like a hunting Thetis (a sea goddess) or a fishing
Diana (goddess of the hunt) as they pursue seals with harpoons.   2 A sea
god who herded seals.   3 Two of the three Fates: Lachesis assigned each
person his or her fate, and Clotho spun the thread of the individual's life.

Rindióse al fin la bestia, y las almenas
de las sublimes rocas salpicando,
las peñas embistió peña escamada,
en ríos de agua y sangre desatada.

Éfire luego—la que en el torcido
luciente nácar te sirvió no poca
risueña parte de la dulce fuente—
de Filódoces émula valiente,
cuya asta breve desangró la foca,
el cabello en estambre azul cogido
—celoso alcaide de sus trenzas de oro—
en segundo bajel se engolfó sola.

¡Cuántas voces le di! ¡Cuántas en vano
tiernas derramé lágrimas, temiendo,
no al fiero tiburón, verdugo horrendo
del náufrago ambicioso mercadante,
     ni al otro cuyo nombre
espada es tantas veces esgrimida
contra mis redes ya, contra mi vida;
sino algún siempre verde, siempre cano
sátiro de las aguas, petulante
violador del virginal decoro,
marino dios, que—el vulto feroz, hombre—
     corvo es delfín la cola.

Sorda a mis voces, pues, ciega a mi llanto,
abrazado, si bien de fácil cuerda,
un plomo fió grave a un corcho leve;
que algunas veces despedido cuanto
—penda o nade—la vista no lo pierda,
el golpe solicita, el bulto mueve

The beast at last surrendered,
and battlements of sublime rocks spattering,
a scale-covered crag charged into the crags,
dissolved in rivers of water and blood.

Efire then—the daughter who in spiraled
gleaming nacre served you no small smiling
   part of the sweet fountain—
valiantly emulates Filódoces[1]   440
whose short harpoon did bleed the bull seal to death,
gathers her hair in a blue woolen net
—jealous guardian of her tresses of gold—
and embarks alone in a small second boat.

   How many cries I uttered!
How many tender tears I shed, fearing
not the savage shark, that horrendous killer
   of the ambitious merchant
shipwrecked, nor the other whose name is sword,
   wielded so often against   450
      my nets, and against my life;
but some ever green, ever hoary satyr[2]
   of the water, a brazen
violator of virginal decorum,
some sea god whose body—his fierce visage a man—
   curves into a dolphin tail.

Deaf to my cries, and blind to the tears I shed,
she trusted heavy lead to lightweight cork
   embracing a slender cord;
   at times it was tossed out   460
as long as—hanging or swimming—she does not
   let it out of her sight,
the splash solicits and the bundle moves

1 Efire and Filódoces are the names of the old fisherman's two daughters. 2 A minor woodland deity associated with Bacchus and sensuality, and usually depicted with a goat's hooves and horns.

prodigïosos moradores ciento
   del líquido elemento.

Láminas uno de viscoso acero
—rebelde aun al diamante—el duro lomo
hasta el luciente bipartido extremo
   de la cola vestido,
solicitado sale del rüido;
y al cebarse en el cómplice ligero
   del suspendido plomo,
480   Éfire, en cuya mano al flaco remo
un fuerte dardo había sucedido,
de la mano a las ondas gemir hizo
el aire con el fresno arrojadizo;
de las ondas al pez, con vuelo mudo,
deidad dirigió amante el hierro agudo:
entre una y otra lámina, salida
la sangre halló por do la muerte entrada.

Onda, pues, sobre onda levantada,
montes de espuma concitó herida
490   la fiera, horror del agua, cometiendo
ya a la violencia, ya a la fuga el modo
   de sacudir el asta,
que, alterando el abismo o discurriendo
   el Océano todo,
no perdona al acero que la engasta.

Éfire en tanto al cáñamo torcido
el cabo rompió, y—bien que al ciervo herido
el can sobra, siguiéndole la flecha—
volvíase, mas no muy satisfecha,
500   cuando cerca de aquel peinado escollo
hervir las olas vió templadamente,
bien que haciendo círculos perfetos;
escogió, pues, de cuatro o cinco abetos
el de cuchilla más resplandeciente,
que atravesado remolcó un gran sollo.

one hundred prodigious huge inhabitants
   of the liquid element.

One in laminas of viscous steel
—a rebel even to the diamond—dressed
along its hard back down to the bipart tail,
   solicited by the noise
comes out and bites the accomplice so lightweight   *470*
   of the suspended lead;
Efire, in whose hand a sturdy dart
   replaced the breakable oar,
from her hand to the waves made the air moan
   with the ash aimed and hurled;
from the waves to the fish, in silent flight,
a deity enamored guided the
sharpened metal: between two laminas
   blood coming out found the place
   where death was going in.   *480*

   Then wave lifted over wave,
mountains of spume the wounded beast, horror
of the water, incited, committed by
   violence or by flight
to shake free of the lance, which, though disturbed be
the abyss or all of Ocean traversed,
will not reprieve the steel embedded there.

Efire meanwhile cut the end of the
twisted hemp, and—though the dog is not needed
behind the wounded stag if the arrow holds—   *490*
   she returned, not satisfied,
   when close to that smooth-faced reef
she saw the waves boil gently, form perfect rounds;
she chose, then, of four or five white firs, the one
   with the most glittering tip,
ran through a great sturgeon, and pulled it in.

Desembarcó triunfando,
y aun el siguiente sol no vimos, cuando
en la ribera vimos convecina
dado al través el monstro, donde apenas
su género noticia, pías arenas
en tanta playa halló tanta rüina.»

Aura en esto marina
el discurso, y el día juntamente,
trémula, si veloz, les arrebata,
alas batiendo líquidas, y en ellas
dulcísimas querellas
de pescadores dos, de dos amantes
en redes ambos y en edad iguales.
　　Dividiendo cristales,
en la mitad de un óvalo de plata,
venía a tiempo el nieto de la espuma
que los mancebos daban alternantes
al viento quejas. Órganos de pluma
　　—aves digo de Leda—
tales no oyó el Caístro en su arboleda,
tales no vió el Meandro en su corriente.
Inficionando pues süavemente
las ondas el Amor, sus flechas remos,
hasta donde se besan los extremos
de la isla y del agua no los deja.

Lícidas, gloria en tanto
de la playa, Micón de sus arenas
　　—invidia de sirenas,
　　convocación su canto
de músicos delfines, aunque mudos—
　　en números no rudos
　　el primero se queja
　　de la culta Leucipe,

510

520

530

She came ashore, triumphant,
and before we saw the next day's sun, we saw
   on the nearby beach, destroyed,
   the monster; no one could say
its kind, there was hardly enough merciful   500
sand to hold so much ruin on so large a beach."

   And here a breeze from the sea
   ended his speech and the day,
      so tremulous, so rapid,
beating liquid wings, bearing the sweet complaints
   of two fishermen, lovers
   equal in nets and in age.
Dividing crystals, in the center of
a silver oval, the grandson of the foam   510
   sailed in[1] as the lads took turns
   singing their plaints to the wind.
Organs of feather—birds worthy of Leda—
the Caystrus never heard among its groves,
Meander never saw along its currents.[2]
Amor, using his arrows as oars, gently
poisons the waves, and stays with the lads until
   the shore, where the ends of the
   island and the water kiss.

   Meanwhile, Lícidas, the glory of the beach,   520
      and Micón[3] of its sands
      —the envy of the sirens,
      their song a convocation
      of dolphins musical though mute—
   in counted not rustic lines
   the first sings his complaint of
   Leucipe the adored,

1 The god Love, or Cupid, son of Venus, daughter of the sea foam, sails in
on a shell of silver.   2 Jupiter came to Leda in the guise of a swan; the rivers
Caystrus and Meander were famous for their swans.   3 Lícidas and Micón
are the names of the two suitors in love with Leucipe and Cloris. Aganippe
was a fountain sacred to the nine Muses.

décimo esplendor bello de Aganipe;
540   de Cloris el segundo,
escollo de cristal, meta del mundo.

LÍCIDAS

    ¿A qué piensas, barquilla,
pobre ya cuna de mi edad primera,
que cisne te conduzgo a esta ribera?
A cantar dulce, y a morirme luego.
    Si te perdona el fuego
que mis huesos vinculan, en su orilla,
tumba te bese el mar, vuelta la quilla.

MICÓN

    Cansado leño mío,
550 hijo del bosque y padre de mi vida
—de tus remos ahora conducida
a desatarse en lágrimas cantando—,
    el doliente, si blando,
curso del llanto métrico te fío,
nadante urna de canoro río.

tenth beautiful splendor of Aganippe;
   of Cloris the second,
reef of crystal, desire of the world.   *530*

LÍCIDAS

   What can you think, little boat,
     poor cradle of my early
days, that like a swan I lead you to this shore
to sweetly sing and then to meet my death?
     If the fire pardons you
that is joined to my bones, on the coastline
     turn up your keel, be my tomb
     as you are kissed by the sea.

MICÓN

   Oh weary craft of mine,
child of the forest and father of my life   *540*
     —by these oars of yours now led
     to melt, singing, into tears—
to you I entrust the sorrowful though sweet
     course of my metered weeping,
floating urn upon a lyrical river.

LÍCIDAS

Las rugosas veneras
—fecundas no de aljófar blanco el seno,
ni del que enciende el mar tirio veneno—
entre crespos buscaba caracoles,
560   cuando de tus dos soles
fulminado, ya señas no ligeras
de mis cenizas dieron tus riberas.

MICÓN

Distinguir sabía apenas
el menor leño de la mayor urca
que velera un Neptuno y otro surca,
y tus prisiones ya arrastraba graves;
si dudas lo que sabes,
lee cuanto han impreso en tus arenas,
a pesar de los vientos, mis cadenas.

LÍCIDAS

570   Las que el cielo mercedes
hizo a mi forma, ¡oh dulce mi enemiga!,
lisonja no, serenidad lo diga
de limpia consultada ya laguna,
y los de mi fortuna
privilegios, el mar a quien di redes,
más que a la selva lazos Ganimedes.

LÍCIDAS

The furrowed scallop shells
—their bosoms not fertile with milky pearls
nor venom that fires the Tyrian sea[1]—
I looked for once among the spiraled shells;
when I was struck by the rays of your two suns   550
these your shores showed clear signs of my ashes.[2]

MICÓN

I could barely distinguish
the smallest boat from the greatest vessel
that swift-sails one Neptune and plows another,
and already I dragged after me your
heavy irons;[3] if you doubt what you know,
read all that has been printed on your sands,
    despite the winds, by my chains.

LÍCIDAS

The grace that heaven granted
    my form, oh sweet enemy!   560
not flattery this but the serene, the clear
reflection seen in the lagoon, and the
privileges of my fortune, the sea to whom I threw
more nets than Ganymede set forest snares.[4]

1 The sea around Tyre, an ancient Phoenician city. 2 That is, he was burned by the two suns of his beloved's eyes. 3 He is, in short, a prisoner of love. 4 Ganymede, supposed to be the most beautiful of mortals, was abducted from Mount Ida by Jupiter to be his cupbearer.

MICÓN

No ondas, no luciente
cristal—agua al fin dulcemente dura—:
invidia califique mi figura
de musculosos jóvenes desnudos.
    Menos dió al bosque nudos
que yo al mar, el que a un dios hizo valiente
mentir cerdas, celoso espumar diente.

LÍCIDAS

Cuantos pedernal duro
bruñe nácares boto, agudo raya
en la oficina undosa desta playa,
tantos Palemo a su Licore bella
    suspende, y tantos ella
al flaco da, que me construyen muro,
junco frágil, carrizo mal seguro.

MICÓN

Las siempre desiguales
blancas primero ramas, después rojas,
de árbol que, nadante, ignoró hojas,
trompa Tritón del agua, a la alta gruta
    de Nísida tributa,
ninfa por quien lucientes son corales
los rudos troncos hoy de mis umbrales.

MICÓN

Not waves, not gleaming crystal
—it is sweetly hardened water after all—
    qualify my figure for
the envy of muscular, naked young men.
Fewer knotted nets than I threw in the sea
were spread in the groves by the one who forced   570
a valiant god bristles to feign, spume of
    tusks, because of jealousy.[1]

LÍCIDAS

All the mother-of-pearl
polished by smooth hard flint, scored by the sharp,
in the undulating workshop of this beach,
these Palemon hangs for his beautiful
    Licore, and she as many
gives to the slim boy,[2] hangs them on my wall
of fragile bulrushes and unsteady reeds.

MICÓN

The ever uneven   580
    branches, first white, then red,
of a tree that, under water, knew no leaves,[3]
Triton,[4] trump of the water, offers to
    the high grotto of Nísida,
nymph for whose sake the rough trunks of my door
    bright corals are today.

1 Venus, loved by Mars, fell in love with the beautiful Adonis. In a jealous
rage, Mars turned himself into a wild boar and gored Adonis to death.   2 Pale-
mon, a sea god, loved the nymph Licore, who loved Lícidas, the "slim
boy."   3 That is, the coral.   4 Triton, a sea god, half man and half fish,
would blow on a trumpet made of shell to calm the sea.

123

LÍCIDAS

Esta, en plantas no escrita,
en piedras sí, firmeza honre Himeneo,
calzándole talares mi deseo:
que el tiempo vuela. Goza, pues, ahora
   los lilios de tu aurora,
que al tramontar del sol mal solicita
abeja, aun negligente, flor marchita.

MICÓN

Si fe tanta no en vano
desafía las rocas donde, impresa,
con labio alterno mucho mar la besa,
nupcial la califique tea luciente.
   Mira que la edad miente,
mira que del almendro más lozano
Parca es interïor breve gusano.

Invidia convocaba, si no celo,
   al balcón de zafiro
las claras, aunque etíopes, estrellas,
   y las Osas dos bellas,
   sediento siempre tiro
del carro perezoso, honor del cielo;
   mas, ¡ay!, que del rüido
   de la sonanta esfera,
a la una luciente y otra fiera
el piscatorio cántico impedido,

600

610

620

LÍCIDAS

May Hymen honor my constancy, writ
  not on plants but on stone,
by placing wingéd sandals on my desire:
  for time flies. Enjoy now   590
  the lilies of your dawn,[1]
for when the sun sets even negligent
bees do not solicit withered flowers.

MICÓN

  If so much faith does not
in vain defy the rocks where, being etched,
the vast sea kisses it with successive lips,
honor it with a flaming nuptial torch.
  Think that the years deceive us,
think that inside the leafiest almond tree
a small worm is its Parca.[2]   600

Envy, if not devotion, summoned to
  the sapphire balcony
  the bright though Ethiope stars
  and the two beautiful Bears,
  ever thirsting, and drawing
the laggard chariot, honor of heaven;[3]
but oh, the clamor of the sounding sphere[4]
  prevented the brilliant beasts
  from hearing the fishers' song,

---

1 He addresses the girl he loves, urging her to agree to marry him. 2 The Parcae are the Fates. 3 Cepheus, the king of Ethiopia, was placed among the stars after his death along with his wife Cassiopea and daughter Andromeda. The Bears are Ursa Major and Ursa Minor, thirsty because, as the result of Juno's punishment, they can never sink into the ocean. 4 That is, the sound of the celestial sphere.

con las prendas bajaran de Cefeo
    a las vedadas ondas,
si Tetis no, desde sus grutas hondas,
    enfrenara el deseo.

¡Oh, cuánta al peregrino el amebeo
alterno canto dulce fué lisonja!
¿Qué mucho, si avarienta ha sido esponja
    del néctar numeroso
630   el escollo más duro?
¿Qué mucho, si el candor bebió ya puro
de la virginal copia en la armonía
el veneno del ciego ingenïoso
que dictaba los números que oía?

Generosos afectos de una pía
doliente afinidad—bien que amorosa
por bella más, por más divina parte—
solicitan su pecho a que, sin arte
    de colores prolijos,
640   en oración impetre ofıcïosa
    del venerable isleño,
que admita yernos los que el trato hijos
    litoral hizo, aún antes
que el convecino ardor dulces amantes.

    Concediólo risueño,
del forastero agradecidamente
y de sus propios hijos abrazado.
Mercurio destas nuevas diligente,
coronados traslada de favores
650   de sus barcas Amor los pescadores
    al flaco pie del suegro deseado.

and they with the darlings of Cepheus   610
would have descended to the forbidden waves
    if Thetis from her deep caves
    had not restrained their desire.

Oh, how the exchange of amoebean[1]
    sweet songs pleased the pilgrim!
But what matter, if even the hardest reef
    was an avid sponge for
    their nectar of harmonies?
What matter, if the pure candor of this
    virginal pair already   620
drank in the harmony poisons of the
clever blind boy dictating the lines he heard?[2]

Generous affections of a compassionate
    sorrowful affinity
—amorous though for one more beautiful,
    more divine—fill his bosom,[3]
    move him in diligent speech
to plead with the venerable islander
that he accept as sons-in-law two whom
    life along the shore had made   630
his sons even before the ardor born
of nearness transformed them into lovers sweet.

And so he grants it, smiling,
as the stranger along with his own children
    embrace him in gratitude.
A diligent Mercury[4] of the news,
Love transports the fishermen, crowned with favors,
    from their boats to the frail feet
    of the father-in-law so long desired.

1 A term that refers to alternating strophes of a verse dialogue. 2 The god Love both dictates the verses (the suitors) and listens to them (the two sisters). 3 The pilgrim's own lost love moves him to plead the case of the suitors. 4 The god Love transforms himself into Mercury, messenger of the gods, who brings the suitors to shore.

¡Oh del ave de Júpiter vendado
pollo—si alado, no, lince sin vista—
político rapaz, cuya prudente
disposición esperuló estadista
 clarísimo ninguno
de los que el reino muran de Neptuno!
¡Cuán dulces te adjudicas ocasiones
para favorecer, no a dos supremos
660   de los volubles polos ciudadanos,
sino a dos entre cáñamo garzones!
¿Por qué? Por escultores quizá vanos
de tantos de tu madre bultos canos
cuantas al mar espumas dan sus remos.
Al peregrino por tu causa vemos
alcázares dejar, donde, excedida
de la sublimidad la vista, apela
 para su hermosura;
 en que la arquitectura
670   a la gëometría se rebela,
jaspes calzada y pórfidos vestida.
Pobre choza, de redes impedida,
 entra ahora, ¡y lo dejas!
¡Vuela, rapaz, y, plumas dando a quejas,
los dos reduce al uno y otro leño,
mientras perdona tu rigor al sueño!

Las horas ya, de números vestidas,
al bayo, cuando no esplendor overo
del luminoso tiro, las pendientes
680   ponían de crisólitos lucientes,
 coyundas impedidas,
mientras de su barraca el extranjero
dulcemente salía despedido
a la barquilla, donde le esperaban
a un remo cada joven ofrecido.

Oh blindfolded fledgling to the bird of   640
Jupiter—or, perhaps, sightless wingéd lynx—
    sagacious boy[1] whose prudent
judgment no illustrious statesman of those
who surround the realm of Neptune has pondered!
What sweet opportunities you award
    to favor not two supreme
    residents of spinning poles[2]
    but two lads among hemp nets!
Why? Perhaps because like sculptors with their oars
they shape fleet forms of your mother born of foam.   650
For your sake we see the pilgrim leave behind
    castles, where sight overcome
by the sublime, calls upon their beauty;
    where architecture rebels
against geometry, wearing shoes of
    jasper, clothes of porphyry.
    Poor hut, crowded with nets
he enters now, and you abandon him!
Take wing, young god, and flying from complaints,[3]
    return them both to their barks   660
    while your rigor allows sleep!

    Now the hours, clad in numbers,
were placing on the bay or golden-haired
    splendor of the shining team[4]
    trappings of gleaming topaz,
    obstructing the harnesses,
    while from his hut the stranger,
    bidden farewell sweetly, left
for the boat where waiting for him the brothers
    each was holding an oar.   670

---

1 The god Love, though blindfolded, has sight as acute as an eagle's, the
bird of Jupiter.   2 That is, the gods who inhabit the poles of the celestial
sphere.   3 The love complaints of the pilgrim.   4 The horses that pull the
chariot of the Sun; it is dawn.

Dejaron, pues, las azotadas rocas
   que mal las ondas lavan
del livor aún purpúreo de las focas,
y de la firme tierra el heno blando
690   con las palas segando,
   en la cumbre modesta
de una desigualdad del horizonte,
   que deja de ser monte
   por ser culta floresta,
antiguo descubrieron blanco muro,
   por sus piedras no menos
que por su edad majestuosa cano;
mármol, al fin, tan por lo pario puro,
que al peregrino sus ocultos senos
700   negar pudiera en vano.
   Cuantas del Océano
   el sol trenzas desata
contaba en los rayados capiteles,
que—espejos, aunque esféricos, fïeles—
bruñidos eran óvalos de plata.

La admiración que al arte se le debe,
áncora del batel fué, perdonando
poco a lo fuerte, y a lo bello nada
   del edificio, cuando
710 ronca los salteó trompa sonante,
   al principio distante,
vecina luego, pero siempre incierta.

   Llave de la alta puerta
el duro son—vencido el foso breve—
levadiza ofreció puente no leve,

And so they left behind the pounded crags
    that the waves have barely washed
of the still livid purple of the seals,
    and with the blades of their oars
mowing the soft grasses of terra firma,[1]
    they saw on a modest rise,
in an unevenness of the horizon
    that is not so much mountain
    as a cultivated grove,
    an ancient white rampart,   680
snowy-headed for its stones no less than for
    its magisterial age;
Parian marble, in short, and so pure
    that in vain would it deny
to the pilgrim the sight of its hidden breast.[2]
    All the tresses that the sun
    loosens rising from Ocean
he counted on the sun-streaked capitals
that—mirrors faithful although spherical—
    were polished silver ovals.   690

    The amazement owed to art
    anchored the boat as they lingered, gazed upon
details of the fortress, and even more,
    details of its beauty, when
the piercing sound of a trumpet startled them,
    distant at first, then closer,
    but ever invisible.

    Key to the high portal
its sharp sound—overpassing the narrow moat—
    a drawbridge, not light, carried   700

1 That is, they are rowing very close to shore. 2 The marble is so pure it is
transparent.

tropa inquïeta contra el aire armada,
lisonja, si confusa, regulada
su orden, de la vista, y del oído
   su agradable rüido.
720   Verde, no mudo coro
   de cazadores era,
cuyo número indigna la ribera.

Al Sol levantó apenas la ancha frente
   el veloz hijo ardiente
   del céfiro lascivo
—cuya fecunda madre al genitivo
soplo vistiendo miembros, Guadalete
florida ambrosia al viento dió jinete—,
que a mucho humo abriendo
730   la fogosa nariz, en un sonoro
relincho y otro saludó sus rayos.
Los overos, si no esplendores bayos,
   que conducen el día,
les responden, la eclíptica ascendiendo.

Entre el confuso, pues, celoso estruendo
de los caballos, ruda hace armonía,
cuanta la generosa cetrería,
desde la Mauritania a la Noruega,
   insidia ceba alada,
740   sin luz, no siempre ciega,
sin libertad, no siempre aprisionada,
   que a ver el día vuelve
las veces que, en fiado al viento dada,
repite su prisión y al viento absuelve.

across a restless troop armed against the air,[1]
pleasing, though confused, in its careful order
    to the eye, and to the ear
    its agreeable din.
    A green,[2] not a silent
    chorus of hunters it was,
    whose numbers irked the shore.

Barely lifting his broad forehead to the Sun,
    the swift ardent son of
    the lascivious zephyr   710
—his fecund mother covering the members
    of the fertilizing breath,
Guadalete offered flowered ambrosia
    to the wind turned into steed[3]—
and opening his spirited nostrils
to the vapor of his breath, in sonorous
repeated whinnies he greeted its rays.
The brilliant horses, golden-haired or bay,
    that draw the day's chariot
answer as the ecliptic they ascend.   720

To the confused and zealous clamoring
of the horses, a rough harmony is formed
    by all the winged astuteness
that creates a bounteous falconry
    from Norway to Mauritane,
    sans light, but not always blind,
sans liberty, but not always in chains,
    they can see the day again
when, offered to the wind in surety,
they return to prison and absolve the wind.   730

---

1 That is, they are hunting birds.   2 Hunting outfits were typically green. The word may also refer to their youth.   3 This extended image evokes the belief that Andalusian horses were fathered by the wind ("lascivious zephyr"), and that the Guadalete River provided them with ambrosia for food.

El neblí, que, relámpago su pluma,
rayo su garra, su ignorado nido,
o lo esconde el Olimpo o densa es nube
    que pisa, cuando sube
tras la garza argentada, el pie de espuma.

750   El sacre, las del noto alas vestido,
sangriento chiprïota, aunque nacido
con las palomas, Venus, de tu carro.

El girifalte, escándalo bizarro
del aire, honor robusto de Gelanda,
si bien jayán de cuanto rapaz vuela,
corvo acero su pie, flaca pihuela
    de piel lo impide blanda.

El baharí, a quien fué en España cuna
del Pirineo la ceniza verde,
760   o la alta basa que el Oceano muerde
    de la egipcia coluna.

    La delicia volante
de cuantos ciñen líbico turbante,
    el borní, cuya ala
en los campos tal vez de Melïona
galán siguió valiente, fatigando
    tímida liebre, cuando
intempestiva salteó leona
    la melionesa gala,
770   que de trágica escena
mucho teatro hizo poca arena.

The falcon that, lightning flash its feathers,
thunder bolt its claws, its nest undisclosed,
hidden by Olympus or the heavy cloud
    it trods with a foot foam light
when it soars after the silvery crane.

The saker, seeming dressed in Notus's wings,
bloodthirsty Cypriot though born among,
    Venus, the doves of your coach.

The gyrfalcon, brave wonder
of the air, of Zeeland[1] stalwart honor,   740
though titan of the flying predators,
its foot curved steel, yet a slender jess of soft
    leather can keep it bound.

The sparrow hawk, whose cradle in Spain was
    green ash of the Pyrenees[2]
or the high base of the Egyptian pillar[3]
    bitten and bruised by Ocean.

The flying delight of all
who wind a Libyan turban,
the marsh harrier, whose wing   750
followed perhaps in fields of Meliona[4]
    a valiant youth exhausting
a timid hare, when a sudden lioness
attacked the gallant Melionian lad,
    and in this tragic scene
made a good deal of theater on little sand.

---

1 Province of the Netherlands, on the North Sea.   2 It was an ancient belief that the Pyrenees were burned in a huge fire (and thence the origin of the name: pyre=Pyrenees).   3 One of the pillars at the Strait of Gibraltar erected by the Egyptian Hercules.   4 An island off the coast of North Africa.

Tú, infestador, en nuestra Europa nuevo,
de las aves, nacido, aleto, donde
entre las conchas hoy del Sur esconde
    sus muchos años Febo,
      ¿debes por dicha cebo?
¿Templarte supo, dí, bárbara mano
al insultar los aires? Yo lo dudo,
que al precïosamente inca desnudo
780   y al de plumas vestido mejicano,
fraude vulgar, no industria generosa,
del águila les dió a la mariposa.

    De un mancebo serrano
el duro brazo débil hace junco,
examinando con el pico adunco
sus pardas plumas, el azor britano,
    tardo, mas generoso
terror de tu sobrino ingenïoso,
ya invidia tuya, Dédalo, ave ahora,
790   cuyo pie tiria púrpura colora.

Grave, de perezosas plumas globo,
que a luz lo condenó incierta la ira
del bello de la estigia deidad robo,
desde el guante hasta el hombro a un joven cela:
esta emulación, pues, de cuanto vuela
por dos topacios bellos con que mira,
    término torpe era
    de pompa tan ligera.

You, osprey, new scourge of birds
in our Europe, born among the shells of the
   Ocean of the South where now
   Phoebus hides his many years,   760
   do you by chance owe your keep?
Did barbarous hand know how to temper you
   when you affronted the air?
I doubt it, since for the naked Inca
adorned in gems, the Mexican dressed in plumes,
vulgar deceit, not bountiful industry,
   granted dominion over
   the eagle, the butterfly.[1]

On the stalwart arm of a mountain lad
   transformed into fragile reed   770
by a British goshawk, scrutinizing
   with curved beak its feathers dark,
   of sluggish but generous flight,
   terror of the shrewd nephew
envied by you, Daedalus, now a bird
   with legs the purple of Tyre.[2]

   Grave globe of lazy feathers,
condemned to uncertain light by the rage
of beauty stolen by the Stygian god,[3]
covers a youth from his shoulder to his glove: 780
   the envy of all that flies,
for the two lovely topazes of its gaze
   put a sluggish ending to
   pomp so agile and quick.

1 The Incas and the Aztecs, in other words, did not train their hunting birds but used the "deceit" of nets to capture the creatures of the air. 2 Daedalus's nephew, variously named Perdix, Talos, or Calos, was almost as inventive as his uncle, who envied him and threw the young man from a tower. Minerva saved him and turned him into a partridge, a bird with red legs. 3 When Pluto, the "Stygian god," abducted Proserpine, Jupiter agreed to let her return to earth if she had not eaten anything in the underworld. Ascalaphus told Jupiter she had consumed six pomegranate seeds, and in revenge Proserpine turned him into an owl.

Can, de lanas prolijo, que animoso
800 buzo será, bien de profunda ría,
   bien de serena playa,
cuando la fulminada prisión caya
   del neblí—a cuyo vuelo,
   tan vecino a su cielo,
el Cisne perdonara, luminoso—,
número y confusión gimiendo hacía
en la vistosa laja para él grave:
que aun de seda no hay vínculo süave.

En sangre claro y en persona augusto,
810   si en miembros no robusto,
príncipe les sucede, abrevïada
en modestia civil real grandeza.
La espumosa del Betis ligereza
bebió no sólo, mas la desatada
majestad en sus ondas, el luciente
caballo que colérico mordía
el oro que süave lo enfrenaba,
arrogante, y no ya por las que daba
estrellas su cerúlea piel al día,
820   sino por lo que siente
de esclarecido y aun de soberano
en la rienda que besa la alta mano,
de cetro digna.

      Lúbrica no tanto
culebra se desliza tortuosa
por el pendiente calvo escollo, cuanto
la escuadra descendía presurosa
por el peinado cerro a la campaña,
que al mar debe con término prescripto
más sabandijas de cristal que a Egipto
830 horrores deja el Nilo que lo baña.

A dog with long hair a bold diver will be,
   either in deep cove waters
   or on a beach serene,
when the lightning-struck prey of the falcon
   falls—the falcon's flight so close
   to its sky that even the   790
   shining Swan must forgive it[1]—
his whimpers added to the clamorous din,
   ornate cord somber to him:
no bond, not even one of silk, can be kind.

With illustrious blood and august person,
   though not robust of limb,
   a prince follows, reducing
his royal grandeur to modest courtesy.
The gleaming horse angrily biting the gold
   that gently restrained him   800
drank not only foaming agility from
Betis[2] but unleashed majesty in its waves;
arrogant, and not only for the stars
his cerulean coat offered to the day
   but for what he senses of
nobility and even sovereignty
in the rein that kisses the high-placed hand,
   worthy of a scepter.

          A lubricious snake
does not slide and coil down the bare rock slope   810
as quickly as the troop descended the tilled
   rise to the plain that the sea
covers to a fixed point, then abandons,
   leaving more crystal vermin[3]
than the horrors the Nile leaves in Egypt,
   the land that its water bathes.

---

1 The constellation Cygnus, also known as the Northern Cross. 2 The Roman name for the river called Guadalquivir by the Moors. 3 The small streams of water left behind by the tide.

Rebelde ninfa, humilde ahora caña,
los márgenes oculta
de una laguna breve,
a quien doral consulta
aun el copo más leve
de su volante nieve.

Ocioso, pues, o de su fin presago,
los filos con el pico prevenía
de cuanto sus dos alas aquel día
840 al viento esgrimirán cuchillo vago.

La turba aun no del apacible lago
  las orlas inquïeta,
que tímido perdona a sus cristales
el doral. Despedida no saeta
de nervios partos igualar presuma
  sus puntas desiguales,
  que en vano podrá pluma
vestir un leño como viste un ala.

Puesto en tiempo, corona, si no escala,
850   las nubes—desmintiendo
su libertad el grillo torneado
que en sonoro metal lo va siguiendo—
  un baharí templado,
  a quien el mismo escollo
—a pesar de sus pinos, eminente—
el primer vello le concedió pollo,
que al Betis las primeras ondas fuente.

No sólo, no, del pájaro pendiente,
las caladas registra el peregrino,
860 mas del terreno cuenta cristalino
    los juncos más pequeños,
verdes hilos de aljófares risueños.

A rebellious nymph, now a humble reed,[1]
obscures the margins of a small lagoon,
    where a kingbird inspects
even the smallest flake of its flying snow.   *820*

Idle, perhaps, or an omen of its end,
it prepared all the edges with its beak
of the blurred knife its two wings will flourish
    against the wind that day.

The crowd has not yet disturbed the banks of the
    tranquil lake whose looking glass
    the timid kingbird forgives.
    No arrow shot by bowstrings
presumes to equal its unequal tips,
for in vain does a feather adorn a shaft   *830*
    as it adorns a wing.

Ready for flight, a crown and not a ladder
    to the clouds—the turned shackle
that in sounding metal pursues, giving
    the lie to its liberty—
    a well-tempered sparrow hawk
to whom the cliffs—eminent despite their pines—
    gave its first down when a chick,
as they gave first waves to Betis when a spring.

Fascinated not by the bird alone,   *840*
    its swooping dives, the pilgrim
ponders the crystalline terrain and counts
    even on the smallest reeds
    green strings of gleaming seed pearls.

1 The nymph Syrinx, fleeing Pan, was turned into a reed, which he then
used as a flute.

Rápido al español alado mira
peinar el aire por cardar el vuelo,
cuya vestida nieva anima un hielo
que torpe a unos carrizos lo retira,
    infïeles por raros,
si firmes no por trémulos reparos.

Penetra, pues, sus inconstantes senos,
    estimándolos menos
    entredichos que el viento;
mas a su daño el escuadrón atento,
expulso lo remite a quien en suma
un grillo y otro enmudeció en su pluma.

Cobrado el baharí, en su propio luto,
o el insulto acusaba precedente,
    o entre la verde hierba
    avara escondía cuerva
purpúreo caracol, émulo bruto
    del rubí más ardiente,
cuando, solicitada del ruïdo,
el nácar a las flores fía torcido,
y con siniestra voz convoca cuanta
    negra de cuervas suma
infamó la verdura con su pluma,
con su número el sol. En sombra tanta
alas desplegó Ascálafo prolijas,
    verde poso ocupando,
    que de césped ya blando,
jaspe lo han hecho duro blancas guijas.

Más tardó en desplegar sus plumas graves
el deforme fiscal de Proserpina,
que en desatarse, al polo ya vecina,
la disonante niebla de las aves;
diez a diez se calaron, ciento a ciento,
    al oro intüitivo, invidïado

He watches the Spanish bird comb rapidly
    the air, waiting to card
the flight of the kingbird whose snowy garb
is moved by icy fear to hide in reeds,
    too few to be relied on,
too tremulous to offer firm defense.   *850*

It enters, then, the reeds' inconstant bosom,
deeming them less forbidden than the wind;
but the troop, intent on harming the bird,
    expels it, sends it to one
that silenced sounding shackles in its plumes.

The sparrow hawk retrieved, in its own mourning
a greedy crow impugned the earlier slight
    or in the green grass blades
hid a scarlet shell, crude simulacrum
    of the most ardent ruby,   *860*
    when, summoned by the noise,
the crow entrusts to flowers the whorled twist of
mother-of-pearl, and with sinister voice calls
in their black totality on all the crows
that with their plumage sully and stain the grass,
with their numbers the sun. In that darkness
    Ascalaphus spread great wings,
    occupying a green mound
of soft grass made hard jasper by small white stones.

Proserpine's deformed accuser needed   *870*
    more time to spread somber wings
than did the dissonant cloud of birds to
    assemble, close to the pole;
by their tens, their hundreds, they fixed upon
    perceptual gold,[1] desired

---

1 So many crows assembled that they seemed to extend to the celestial
poles; they were attracted by the golden eyes of the owl.

deste género alado,
si como ingrato no, como avariento,
que a las estrellas hoy del firmamento
900   se atreviera su vuelo
en cuanto ojos del cielo.

Poca palestra la región vacía,
de tanta invidia era,
mientras, desenlazado la cimera,
restituyen el día
a un girifalte, boreal arpía,
que, despreciando la mentida nube,
a luz más cierta sube,
cenit ya de la turba fugitiva.

910   Auxilïar taladra el aire luego
un duro sacre, en globos no de fuego,
en oblicuos sí engaños
mintiendo remisión a las que huyen,
si la distancia es mucha:
griego al fin. Una en tanto, que de arriba
descendió fulminada en poco humo,
apenas el latón segundo escucha,
que del inferïor peligro al sumo
apela, entre los trópicos grifaños
920   que su eclíptica incluyen,
repitiendo confusa
lo que tímida excusa.

Breve esfera de viento,
negra circunvestida piel, al duro
alterno impulso de valientes palas,
la avecilla parece,
en el de muros líquidos que ofrece
corredor el diáfano elemento

by this winged genre not
through ingratitude[1] but greed,
for they would dare fly today to the stars
in the firmament, the eyes of heaven.

The empty region was a small arena   *880*
    for so much envy, and then,
    removing the leather hood,
the hunters restore day to a gyrfalcon,
northern harpy, that scorns the deceptive cloud,
    climbs to a more certain light,
the zenith now to the fugitive crowd.

    Then an aide pierces the air,
a powerful saker, not in balls of fire[2]
    but in oblique deceptions
feigning remission to those birds that flee   *890*
if the distance between them is great: in short,
a Greek.[3] One of many rooks that from on high
descended like a bolt with little smoke
as soon as it heard the second sound of brass
that from the lower danger calls to the
    higher, between the hawkish
tropics that include its ecliptical path
    repeating in confusion
    what it timidly excused.[4]

    A small sphere of wind, covered   *900*
in black skin, subject to hard alternating
strikes by valiant clubs, is what the small bird seems
between fluid walls that offer a running
path in the transparent element for twin

---

1 According to an adage, "Raise crows and they'll peck out your eyes." 2 The *sacre* or saker was the name of a cannon as well as a hunting bird. 3 In other words, astute. 4 The crow is caught between the gyrfalcon above and the saker below, and flies back and forth between them like the sun follows its eclipsis between the tropics.

al gémino rigor, en cuyas alas
930   su vista libra toda el extranjero.

Tirano el sacre de lo menos puro
desta primer región, sañudo espera
la desplumada ya, la breve esfera,
que, a un bote corvo del fatal acero,
dejó al viento, si no restituído,
heredado en el último graznido.

Destos pendientes agradables casos
vencida se apeó la vista apenas,
que del batel, cosido con la playa,
940   cuantos da la cansada turba pasos,
        tantos en las arenas
el remo perezosamente raya,
a la solicitud de una atalaya
atento, a quien doctrina ya cetrera
        llamó catarribera.

Ruda en esto política, agregados
tan mal ofrece como construídos
bucólicos albergues, si no flacas
        piscatorias barracas,
950   que pacen campos, que penetran senos,
        de las ondas no menos
        aquéllos perdonados
que de la tierra éstos admitidos.

Pollos, si de las propias no vestidos,
de las maternas plumas abrigados,
vecinos eran destas alquerías,
mientras ocupan a sus naturales,
Glauco en las aguas, y en las hierbas Pales.

¡Oh cuántas cometer piraterías
960   un cosario intentó y otro volante
—uno y otro rapaz digo milano—,

cruelties, on whose wings
the stranger's eyes are fixed.

The saker, tyrant of the
less pure region, waits, brutal
for the small sphere, despoiled at the curved blow
of fatal steel that left to the wind, if not   910
returned, the inheritance of its last croak.

From these pleasant, unresolved
events no sooner had he looked away
in the small boat, very close to the beach,
than the weary troop takes as many steps on
        sands as the lazy oar strokes,
attentive to the lookout's solicitude,
called falconer in the lore of falconry.

And now rough courtesy offers to view
rustic shelters or crumbling fishermen's huts   920
placed together as poorly as they are built,
grazing the fields, penetrating the coves,
the first forgiven by the waves no less
than the second are admitted by the land.

Chicks, if in their own not dressed,
sheltered by maternal plumes,
        dwell in these hovels while
their owners are occupied by Glaucus
in the waters, by Pales in the grasses.[1]

Oh, how many piracies   930
did one flying corsair and another
attempt—I mean the ravening goshawks—

---

1 Glaucus was a marine divinity with prophetic powers; Pales was the
patron of herds.

bien que todas en vano,
contra la infantería, que piante
en su madre se esconde, donde halla
voz que es trompeta, pluma que es muralla.

A media rienda en tanto el anhelante
caballo—que el ardiente sudor niega
en cuantas le densó nieblas su aliento—
a los indignos de ser muros llega
céspedes, de las ovas mal atados.

Aunque ociosos, no menos fatigados,
quejándose venían sobre el guante
los raudos torbellinos de Noruega.
Con sordo luego estrépito despliega
—injuria de la luz, horror del viento—
sus alas el testigo que en prolija
desconfianza a la sicana diosa
dejó sin dulce hija,
y a la estigia deidad con bella esposa.

although all were in vain
against the infantry that peeps and chirps,
hiding under their mother, where they find
a voice like a trumpet, feathers that are walls.

Meanwhile, at a fast canter, the panting
horse—denying ardent perspiration
   in dense clouds of heaving breath—   940
comes to sod badly tied by algae and
   indignant at being walls.

   Though idle, no less fatigued,
   on the glove came complaining
the rapid whirlwinds from Norway.[1] Then with
   silent clamor the witness
—an affront to the light, horror of the wind—
spreads its wings, one who left the Sicanian
goddess[2] in long-lived doubt bereft of her sweet
child, the Stygian god with a lovely bride.

---

[1] That is, the hawks.   [2] The owl, in betraying Proserpine, deprived Ceres,
the Sicanian goddess, of her daughter.